Taoist Alchemy

&

Breathing Practice:

DIRECT INSTRUCTIONS
FOR THE FIVE BREATHINGS

(Wuxi Zhi Zhi)

Translated from the Classical Chinese
Original Text and Annotated

Dan KJ Vercammen

with an Introduction to the Practice

Antwerp, Belgium, 2023

ISBN: 979-8-35091-721-5 paperback

ISBN: 979-8-35091-722-2 ebook

The author and publisher advice against practicing any of the exercises described in the text without the guidance and/or supervision of a competent teacher and cannot be held responsible for any accident or other issue occurring because of the reader's actions.

Cover image: Longevity of Cranes and Pine Trees, painting by Ren Bonian (1840 – 1896), from the author's collection

www.7starsstudio.shop
www.taoiststudies.org

CONTENTS

A Few Words …

The origin of this book can be found in Shanghai in the middle of the 1980s. A lot of time has passed since then. For many reasons, this has always been a very demanding book to write.

My experience with and knowledge of the subject of this book comes from many sources. I am very grateful to all my internal alchemy and *qigong* teachers for what they taught me, but I am equally indebted to all those practitioners and writers of the past generations whom I have come to know through their works and the other "interactions" I have had with them.

The first edition of this book was a limited insider's one and so, too few people got to know this publication. We intend to reach a wider audience with this volume. It deserves an audience and attention, because it presents some of the backgrounds and also practices that each and every practitioner of qigong and Chinese internal alchemy should be acquainted with.

I want to thank Wenshan and my late wife, An Woestenborghs, for their practical help with the first edition, but this edition wouldn't have seen the light without the support of my present partner, Angela Verkade, whom I'm very grateful to.

Antwerp, Winter 2023

The Five Breathings: a Personal Story

I have a long personal relationship with this text. When I was doing research for my PhD thesis on Chinese internal martial arts (*neijiaquan*) and qigong in Shanghai back in 1985-6, one of my main teachers/informants was Shen Hongxun (1939-2011), a taijiquan and qigong teacher who had invented a qigong system that he called *taiji wuxigong*. The name "*taiji wuxigong*" can be translated as "the five breathings exercise of *Taiji*". Its method consists of two main parts.[1] One part consists of eight basic exercises, each of which is supposed to induce a special kind of breathing (head, shoulder, chest, belly, and heel breathing). The movements of these exercises were derived from the Yang tradition of taijiquan.

---

[1] See his Chinese book on *Taiji Wuxigong*, which he wrote in collaboration with his wife Dr. Xia Tingyu: *Taiji Wuxigong* (published by Taiji Wuxigong Yanjiuhui [Research Association], s.l., s.d.).

Shen had learned this style of taijiquan from Yue Huanzhi (1899-1961), who taught at Zhendan University and Catholic Middle School in Shanghai.[2] The other part is a standing exercise or *zhanzhuang*, which generates so-called *zifa donggong* or spontaneous movements. When practicing this stance (also derived from Yang style taijiquan's initial posture) most people start to experience vibrations after a while, but these may expand to an almost unlimited number of very diverse and sometimes very peculiar movements. By means of his/her suggestive skills the teacher also influences the student to create even more movements and in this way the teacher transmits some of his/her knowledge. This system also uses a taijiquan method and knowledge (namely the releasing of *neijin* or internal energies). The energies are closely connected with the qi-circulations in the body and the student learns how this *qi* can be sent out (by which the internal version actually becomes an external one). My first impressions of a Chinese breathing practice based on five types of breathings came from *taiji wuxigong*.[3]

---

[2] After the Communist take-over in 1949 its name changed to Fudan. This school not only comprised a Middle School but also a University. As a postgraduate student I studied Classical Chinese Philosophy at Fudan University in 1985-86. More information on Yue can be found here: http://ymaa.com/articles/ymaa-taijiquan-lineage.

[3] In 1987 Shen Hongxun and I discussed the suitability of this name for his system. He had given it the prefix of "*taiji*" because he had developed the exercises out of *taijiquan* movements. However, because he had mainly lived and practiced in Xinjiang, he liked to call it "Tianshan Style *wuxigong*", after the beautiful Tianshan (Heavenly Mountains) in this remote Chinese region. I knew of at least two other qigong and/or martial arts systems that were called "Tianshanpai (Heavenly Mountains Style)" and dissuaded him from using this name to avoid confusion. Shen also self-published a booklet on his qigong exercises under the title *Tianshan Wuxigong* (s.l., s.d.).

My experience with Taoist breathing was very different from what I had observed during my practice of yoga from 1972 onwards.[4]

Shen was, in a way, a typical example of a qigong teacher who had developed his own system out of older techniques, and in another way he was atypical, because he seemed to be very interested in research into both the ancient traditions and the modern scientific ways. Of course, he was supposed to be interested in research and modernization, because this was part of what Deng Xiaoping had in mind for the New China he and his comrades were creating. Anyway, Shen was willing to contribute his knowledge to my research and seemed a suitable informant. So, in order to be able to perform my *neijiaquan* and qigong research in the most thorough way, I became his first foreign *tudi*, his inside disciple. During the years we collaborated (1985-1987) I was able to learn his taijiquan, qigong and medical skills from him. I also provided him with the opportunity to go abroad, inviting him to come and live with me in Ghent (Belgium) on my expense, so that we could work closely together on the research of taijiquan and qigong. My PhD thesis promotor, professor Charles Willemen, needed some persuasion to accept Shen as a voluntary researcher for one academic year at his Sinology department, because this would-be researcher had not done any real research and was not a published scientific author. But eventually Willemen agreed to let him come, because, after all, I was paying for him and his information was supposed to be beneficial to my research.

---

[4] The main difference is that in my practice of Taoist breathing things happen naturally, spontaneously and in that way are not "learned" but "discovered" or "recovered".

Shen and I collaborated from January till October 1987, teaching and practicing both taiji wuxigong and taijiquan. Early November we decided to go our separate ways, mainly because Shen's ambitions had changed and I didn't fit into his plans anymore.

As I have mentioned above, Shen's qigong system was rooted in his experience with Yang Tradition (or Dong Yingjie lineage) taijiquan, which he had studied with Yue Huanzhi. He spiced the system with some Lamaist theory (learned from Fahai Lama, according to his saying)[5] and some Taoist philosophy and practices, most of which came from the Longmenpai (Dragon Gate Tradition of Quanzhen [Complete Authenticity] Taoism), to which, according to his words, his grandfather, Shen Baotai, belonged. The name of his method, he said, came from the *Wuxi Chan Wei* text, which, because of loss of his family's property during the twentieth century turmoil in China, was not in his possession anymore.

In order to study what I then thought was the origin of his knowledge, I wanted to go looking for the text. I found a copy in Shanghai's library and took a brief look at it. At first glance, there seemed to be interesting information in it. Because my time was limited on that first visit to the library, I decided to go back later and have the text copied. Great was my surprise the second time that they could not find the text! It seemed as if the ancient practice of having to knock thrice at a teacher's door in order to be allowed in, was also playing tricks with me wanting to get into the contents of

---

[5] For more information about Fahai Lama and his teachings, see Monica Esposito (2008), pp. 473-548.

the text. The third time that I went there, they did find the text, in fact they found two: one named *Wuxi Chan Wei* (*Explanation of the Details of the Five Breathings*) and one named *Wuxi Zhi Zhi* (*Direct Instructions for the Five Breathings*). The first version is the bare text without commentaries, whereas the second one includes commentaries. The text with the commentaries was annotated and published in Shanghai by the alchemical study group surrounding the famous alchemist- scholar Chen Yingning (1880-1969).[6] From what I know now, I assume that Shen's grandfather, who was living in the same (French) concession in Shanghai as Chen Yingning was when the text was published, probably purchased or borrowed and studied it.

Except for the similarity between part of the title of the *Wuxi Zhi Zhi* text and the name of Shen's qigong system, there is very little connection between the two items. Shen Hongxun's theory of qigong contained some influence of Taoist and Buddhist philosophy and medicine, and so does the text, but that influence is obviously not coming from the same sources. In fact, the text is mainly a theoretical exposé about the changes one's breathing goes through during the practice of Taoist internal alchemy and it only briefly mentions some of the most commonly known practices, such as counting breath and regulating breath. In this text, these practices seem to be deliberately and actively induced methods, whereas Shen's system mainly relies on spontaneous evolution, spontaneously arising motion, and manipulation of the student by

---

[6] A very informative book on Chen Yingning is *Daoist Modern* by Xun Liu (2009).

the teacher. To say that Shen's system is rooted in this text tradition is therefore absurd.

Back in 1986, I translated this text for the first time, thinking I might need it for my PhD research. When it dawned upon me that the text itself was not of great importance to my research, because it could not be linked to *neijiaquan*, the internal martial arts, I decided not to use it. My then girlfriend, student and younger disciple under Shen, Monica Esposito (1962-2011), as a result came up with the idea to base her MA dissertation on the research of this text and of Shen's qigong system, and I offered to help her translate the text into Italian, using my English translation as a guide. We also tried to find out as much as possible about the text and its presumed author, but very little could be found. For Monica, it was the start of an ongoing pursuit, taking her on a long time investigation of the Longmenpai and Taoist texts, and also of the story and practices of Fahai Lama (see Esposito [1995] and [2008]).

Was it a coincidence that I decided to start translating the text anew in the year when both of these people died? In any case, these unfortunate circumstances created an opportunity to commemorate them with this publication and thank them posthumously for the things we shared, practiced, and investigated together. Let us say that the text reminds me of many happy days in the good old Shanghai of 1985-86.

Dan K.J. Vercammen, Winter 2013

Introduction

The Text and its Contents

Breathing and Taoist Alchemy
An Inseparable Couple

The translated text presented in this volume is clearly influenced by the three main traditions of China: (Neo-)Confucianism, Buddhism and Taoism. That is obvious for anyone who has some knowledge about these traditions. However, whereas Buddhism and Confucianism mainly serve the role of "supporting cast", the main character is Taoist alchemy, and more precisely the use of breath in this practice.

Taoist alchemy has a long history and comes from several sources, including metallurgy, Chinese Medicine, Taoist health practices and rituals, and more. In Taoism, the practice of alchemy has always been regarded as a superior yet difficult way to reach Dao, the Way. It transforms the body of the alchemist and its potential in such a way that the alchemist who succeeds, transcends the worldly and human conditions and becomes a *Xian*, an "Immortal". In order to make this happen, the alchemists of ancient times made good use of "medicinal" recipes that contained metals, minerals, and herbs. But, they also used their own body, and specifically made use of something that can be found inside the body, yet also outside of it: qi. Etymological dictionaries will explain qi as basically that which creates clouds, a vapor.[7] In man, this is breath. Outside of man, it becomes that which permeates the entire universe and holds it together, while creating its transformations. If one wants to understand Taoist alchemy, one needs to know about qi. And the best way to do this may be to study and practice breathing. In that way, this text about the Five Breathings directly hits the mark.

Until our last breath, we all are breathing all the time. There is nothing we can do about it, it just happens. In fact, we do not actually breathe ourselves, but receive our breath from the cosmos and are forced to return it to its source. And then, one day, it is taken away from us. When left without, we die. Some people

---

[7] See Michael Stanley-Baker's text on qi: https://www.academia.edu/39695488/2019_Qi_in_Critical_Terms_for_Religious_Studies.

experience the "help" of other beings in taking away their breath, but most of us die a more peaceful death.

While we are alive and breathing, we usually don't do much with it. It is much more common for people to injure their breath than to improve on it. Much breath is lost, does not reach the fullest extent of its power, because we, mostly unconscious of what we are doing, do not open up enough and resist the force of breath. Taoists and alchemists call this phenomenon "*fanxi*' or "the breathing of the common people". Through experiments with breathing they knew that more can be done with deeper breathing than most humans assume. They refer for evidence to the writings of, for instance, the early Taoist Zhuangzi (5th - 4th century BCE), who proclaims there exists something like a heel breathing, which is the breathing of the Authentic (Wo)man.[8] This led/leads them to pursue this heel breathing and to reach the goal of *Zhen* or Authenticity, for one's Authenticity is closely linked with using one's full human potential.[9]

---

[8] See the translation by Burton Watson of the ancient Taoist text *Zhuangzi*, available on the internet: http://terebess.hu/english/chuangtzu.html. Heel breathing is mentioned in the first part of chapter 6.

[9] Authenticity or *zhen* is a characteristic of a Taoist alchemist, who is therefore called an Authentic (Wo)man *(Zhenren)*. Several meanings and ideas are connected with this denomination. In Taoist alchemical context, it denotes someone who has succeeded in his/her practice (the practice itself is often called "developing and restoring Authenticity"). But, it also involves seeing through all that is false and understanding what is true and authentic. A *Zhenren* is devoid of illusions. The Embryo that grows in the alchemist's body shall eventually emerge as a *Zhenren*, a newborn person, who connects with the *Dao* or the Way. See, for instance, the *Daojiao Da Cidian*, p. 791, for a list of meanings of *Zhenren*. Some Western scholars call *zhenren* a "perfected or realized person"; see F. Pregadio and L. Skarr in Kohn (2000): p. 481.

Millennia of Taoist and alchemical practice in China (and of other practices in other cultural regions) have provided the human world with countless ways of practicing different kinds of breathing. To keep things simple, let us just stay with the Chinese views and practices. Breath or qi is regarded as something that is not limited to human breath, but in fact permeates all and everything. The whole of the cosmos is full of qi and all changes and evolutions in the cosmos and in everything and everyone that exist in there, are due to it. All processes inside our body are driven by it. In order to perform these actions, qi, of course, changes all the time. These changes, i.e. the ordinary ones that we all share, happen spontaneously and enable us to live and display all the capacities that we have. But, since there must be more, according to the Chinese breath specialists, more subtle changes are also possible and should be realized. There are several ways to make these changes possible. Some insist that one should guide one's breath by using focus and movements in order to create transformation; others say that things occur spontaneously, if one is able to not withstand the power of Heaven and Earth and let Nature do its work; still others do long and tedious workouts in order to achieve deeper breathing; and some combine all sorts of practices to make sure they get there.

From my own experience, I tend to support the "natural" or "spontaneous" evolution. When I was twelve, I started doing yoga and *pranayana* breathing techniques. It made me realize that breathing could indeed behave differently by changing body posture and forcing it to move in a different way. However, the results disappeared soon after I had stopped the exercise. Later, when I went to China and studied qigong, I found out that, by combining exercises that change the body posture and the way the body moves with a practice called "sitting and forgetting"[10], my breathing went through many different transformations. Moreover, these transformations also created a lasting condition of deeper breathing. One day, I also experienced what heel breathing meant, when my heels literally felt like breathing (a similar sensation as breathing through the nostrils or mouth). A state of hibernation (hardly any breathing and heart beat) was another experience that was new to me then. All my experiences led me to believe that without interfering much with breathing, it can do many things that it does not do in an ordinary condition. I do not mean that one does not have to do much, on the contrary, long and diligent practice is of the utmost importance, but the changes in breathing should come by interfering less with breathing (and other things we try to control or think about too much) and not with more control based on thought or imagination. The moment we start to *think* that we should breathe in this or that way and we try to *force* our bodies to "help" breathing (by, for instance, leading qi along a real or imaginary path), we are, in my humble opinion, on the wrong track. What we should do is make our bodies ready to receive and return breath in the least interfering and humble way, meaning that we should learn that Heaven and Earth (i.e. the cosmos) know better and we should not resist what they have in mind for us. This may sound fatalistic, but, in fact, it is quite the opposite.

---

[10] A practice that Zhuangzi refers to. In Chinese it is called "*zuowang*".

By doing so, we can aim at becoming (an active part of) Heaven and Earth and sharing in their possibilities (such as long life). This is an implication of the process of what the Taoists and alchemists call "joining with the Way *(hedao)*".

It is clear from the text that the transformation of breathing, leading to the five types of breathing mentioned, is considered (by the author of the text) to be the essence of Taoist alchemical practice. One should bear in mind that this means there can be no valuable results if these changes do not occur. To make them occur, in my view, two main roads are available. One is suggested in the text, namely: starting out from the practice of the counting of breath and then regulating it, one gradually enters the state of spontaneous breath transformations, leading to the spontaneous experience of heel breathing, embryonic breathing, and united primary breathing. Original breathing is also mentioned, but not clearly explained. The other way works by dropping the counting and regulating and immediately using the method of sitting and forgetting to have the breathing evolve spontaneously into the types mentioned. In this case, it is necessary to stress that the body still needs means to get into this state. To provide these means, other ways of practicing must be pursued first: internal martial arts, Taoist health practices, Taoist diets, and so on. The healthier the body is when doing sitting and forgetting, the less problems the practitioner shall experience when practicing tranquil sitting. As a person involved in the realization of Authenticity, I wish to stress that the mere practice of so-called internal martial arts or Taoist practices does not lead to the necessary results. Getting

14

there is based on *how* you practice, not on what you practice, and unfortunately, very few people seem to know how to practice. The pursuit of illusions is more harmful than you can imagine, so, be careful when you choose a teacher. Results should be actually there and reveal themselves. Your body and the way it functions will be really different after going through the transformation of breath. You will think, feel and act differently. Your body will react differently to what you eat, what you do to or with it, and so on. This may have huge consequences that influence not only yourself, but also your surrounding, and especially the person(s) you share your life with. Be warned and do not engage in this practice recklessly. As the changes that one goes through are different for each and every individual, it is impossible to give you a general account of things. You need an experienced teacher to guide you.

The Five Breathings

A Brief Critical View of the Text's Contents

Reading the text, we can ask ourselves what the five breathings actually are. After all, the text writes about more than five breathing topics: Ordinary Breathing, Observing Breathing, Counting Breath, Regulating Breath, Heel Breathing, Embryonic Breathing, United Primary Breathing, and Original Breathing. Of these eight topics, Counting, Regulating, Heel, Embryonic, and United Primary Breathing are considered to be Five Methods. This may lead one to conclude that these must then be the Five Breathings mentioned in the title. Whether they are all methods can be questioned. In fact, the real method is observing. Counting and Regulating are just techniques. That leaves us with a different view: Ordinary,

Heel, Embryonic, United Primary, and Original should be the Five Breathings. The first of these (Ordinary Breathing) you already have, the others are the result of diligent practice. The differences between the last four are obscure, when you read the text carefully. Heel Breathing seems to take up a very prominent place and in some instances is quintessential. The Original Breathing can be seen as an alternative to develop the Heel-, Embryonic, and Primary United Breathings and is therefore not really yet another breathing. So, the most obvious conclusion is that the Five Methods are to be taken as the Five Breathings.

Because the actual method is spontaneous, once the techniques of counting and regulating are learned, one can only observe the changes and experience the types of breathing that occur. But the author of the Chinese text does not mention this important information clearly. Therefore, the reader is left without a clue about how to proceed. The author seems not to be very helpful as far as showing the way to practice. In this, he is no different from most Taoist writers who do not reveal the real secrets, out of fear that the method may be abused. He quotes from older texts when ways of practicing are concerned, albeit sometimes less explicit than the older originals.[11] His descriptions of the transformations of breath are often vague, obscure and highly theoretical. This may indicate that the author himself did not experience them in

---

[11] Techniques such as regulating breath were explained in detail in, for instance, the Song text compilation *Yun Ji Qiqian* (*Book Case of the Clouds with Seven Labels*). See also Maspero (1971): pp. 373-9 for a description of part of the contents of Taoist texts on breathing.

person and is describing what his teacher(s) told him.[12] Yet again, he may also just want to wet the appetite and lead the reader to further study and reading. In any case, without proper guidance the reader (and especially the Western reader) may be at a loss.

What makes this text worth studying is the fact that it distinguishes more types of breathing than other texts that preceded it. There exist several texts about Embryonic Breathing[13] and these indicate that this is the goal of Taoist breathing practice. To list United Primary Breathing as a further stage is unusual. The order in which they appear makes it obvious that the United Primary Breathing is caused by further refining of breath, once Embryonic Breathing is obtained. Whether it should bear a different name is a matter of choice and the author has made the choice to differentiate further. This makes him and his text special. From the commentaries by Chang Zunxian[14], we can observe that when he rediscovered the text and started studying it, he also found it to be confusing in some parts. Still he made it publicly available, because of its unusual and more explicit treatment of Taoist

---

[12] This was/is a very common practice in China. Copying information from written and oral sources without giving credit to the original sources is also customary.

[13] These can also be found in the *Yun Ji Qiqian* and the *Taoist Canon*. See Schipper and Verellen (2004), especially on pp. 27-8 for information about the *Yun Ji Qiqian* and its author. See pp. 352 ff. for information on the texts concerning breathing exercises.

[14] Chang Zunxian belonged to the circle of Chen Yingning (1880-1969), the influential Taoist scholar and alchemist, who was responsible for a revival of interest in Taoist alchemy in the twentieth century. See notes to the preface of the translated text for Chang Zunxian. For the importance of Chen Yingning and his alchemical circle see Liu (2009). Chang is mentioned there on pp. 7-8 and elsewhere. A photograph of Chang is on p. 183.

breathing. And for sure, it definitely deserves a place in Taoist alchemical literature, as an elaboration of an important theme in Taoist practice: the refining of breath.

The Stages of Breathing

Order and Chaos

When one starts practicing Taoist breathing several phenomenons can be observed. Some guidelines also need to be observed. The translated text mentions some, yet leaves some unmentioned. In order to help the reader to take on the practice, we shall describe the most important issues below.

Taoist alchemical masters and experts on breathing practice always stress that the practice should be done in proper order. However, the practice also contains a fair deal of chaos, because, once the spontaneous process takes over, things not necessarily happen in a fixed order.

It is important to follow a certain orderly routine to avoid problems along the way. The text shows this by discussing *rushou* or initial techniques before continuing with the spontaneous evolution. In this case, the reader is shown how to sit and how to start the breathing practice (by counting the breath). A more elaborate and safer way of practicing is discussed in this book after the translation of the original text.[15] Next in the translated text comes the description of the condition the practitioner starts from, being that of ordinary breathing. It is indeed important to make the practitioner aware of his/her condition and that this is what (s)he has and needs to work with. All stages of the practice are concerned with observation of what happens, a state of not interfering by means of thought or imagination while experiencing the transformations caused by linking focus and breath. Therefore, a short yet powerful section is devoted to this method.[16] It is also stressed that this method is not only used by Taoists, but is essentially the way the Buddhists (of the Tiantai Tradition) practice. Then follow the two techniques that need some actual doing: counting and regulating breath. The author reminds the reader that these should be acquired in order to continue with the further developments. These developments will reveal themselves, after mastering the fundamental techniques, as phenomenons of the refinement of breath, bringing about actions inside the body and mind (such as the sensation of qi rising through the back of the

---

[15] See chapter "Taoist Breathing Exercises".

[16] The importance of this section also transpires from the length of the commentary added.

body and descending in chest and belly). The last thing one reads is a big warning. One should not practice recklessly and be virtuous and good, so as not be reprimanded or punished for one's bad conduct. So, what we learn is that we need to proceed in order and work on our conduct, if we don't want to fail.

A brief look at the stages a practitioner goes through should be helpful. When you start, not much of interest happens. At least, that is how it seems. You first must find the right conditions (meaning place and position, in the first place) to practice. If these are not right yet, you will know: your body starts to "misbehave" (your back hurts, you get distracting thoughts, you feel uncomfortable). Once conditions are more adequate, a calm enters, thoughts diminish. Meanwhile the body becomes internally active: in the abdomen something is stirring (it gets warmer there, you experience movement, vibrations). Concentration and observation start to improve and you can experience all kinds of phenomenons you probably never experienced before (observation of colors, sounds, visions, breathing gets heavier, lighter, faster, longer, ...; more movements inside the body leading to external movements that may become numerous and big). This is a precarious situation in which things can go badly wrong and you need a good teacher to help you through this stage (otherwise you may go mad or become seriously ill)! The order in which things happen can be different from one individual to the other. Some chaos must be allowed for! After going through a lot of these phenomenons for quite some time (months or years), these seem to disappear again, becoming very faint. A very profound sense or state of tranquillity happens.

You don't know where you are, who you are, there is no "you" anymore. You gain all kinds of insights. Life is joyful and worth living and full of interesting things. There is a condition you can always find inside yourself where all is peaceful, quiet, and at rest. You feel satisfied, not wanting any thing. Your breathing is very subtle and self-regulating. It is omnipresent in all functions of your body and enhances your health. You are much less dragged along by circumstances and instead find ways to create harmonious circumstances and change disharmonious ones. Stability and firmness are there to enjoy and you have found yourself and your way. Intuition, insight, and creative ideas prevail over deliberate and ordinary thoughts. People who search harmony come looking for you and those inclined to disharmony start avoiding you. Physically, there are also some signs that can be observed (your skin, one of the largest instruments of breath, for instance, changes: it becomes softer and gives you a youthful look).

There are two main roads available when this has been realized. One is the continuation of the individual practice, the other is its temporary discontinuation. If and when the practitioner decides the time to withdraw from the world has not yet come and (s)he feels the need to make other people share in the wonders of the practice, (s)he will engage in a social life that is all about making sure that the right people gain access to the practice and its results. The practitioner then becomes a teacher, a practitioner of medicine, a writer and the like. With this choice the practitioner puts himself/herself in the middle of life and its chores, problems, and usual circumstances, which then become the material to work with, so that a more harmonious world may result from this work. If and when the practitioner decides to take the second option, (s)he withdraws from the world, (s)he solely practices the refinement of breath and does nothing else except complete the process.

Usually, this last choice is the one the practitioner takes when worldly circumstances are not at all beneficial to the development of Taoist alchemy or when (s)he has reached a ripe old age.

Of course, the above is just a short introduction to the stages and phenomenons. Again, I must point the reader in the direction of an experienced teacher to learn more and study under favorable conditions. The practical exercises given at the end of this book, however, can be used for the initial practice.

Direct Instructions for the Five Breathings

(Translated from the Original Classical Chinese Text by
Dan K.J. Vercammen)

Edited Original Preface

to the

Explanation of the Obscurities

in the

Direct Instructions for the Five Breathings

The source of ancient health practices must be traced back to the *Book of Yinyang Changes*. Kongzi[17] called the continuous produc-

---

[17] Kongzi (Confucius), the best known Chinese philosopher, is traditionally seen as the author of commentaries to the *Yijing* or *Classic of the Yinyang Changes*. About the "continuous production" see Song (1935): p. 281. In C.F. Baynes' English translation (1978[10]) of R. Wilhelm's German translation it can be found on p. 299.

tion "Changes". The beginning of the Changes is the revolving of sun and moon. They invigorate themselves without ever stopping (*xi*).[18] Zisi[19] said: "What does not stop endures." Mengzi[20] said: "That which receives breath by day and night," but this receiving breath is the way of exchange and connection between Heaven and man. When it is put in order, one obtains life; when it is maltreated, one dies because of it. This is the one critical issue in the existence of man. Wang Shuhe's *Classic of Difficult Issues*[21] says: "In man's breathing, one expiration and one inspiration make one breathing [movement] (*xi*)."[22] Daytime and nighttime combined, that makes thirteen thousand five hundred breathing movements. During one breathing movement, the sun in the sky moves more than five hundred and thirty thousand *li*.[23] One cannot investigate Heaven entirely in its most vast and highest extent. The empty void between what is below Heaven and above

---

[18] One meaning of the character "*xi*" is "to breathe", another is "to stop". The next few quotes are all about "*xi*", but it needs to be translated in English as either "breath(ing)" or "stop(ping)", whereas in Chinese it carries different meanings at the same time.

[19] Zisi was Kongzi's grandson. The quote comes from the *Zhongyong* (*Doctrine of the Mean*) 26; see: http://ctext.org/liji/zhong-yong.

[20] Mengzi (or Mencius as he is known to the West) was a Confucian philosopher and writer from the 4th - 3rd century BCE. This quote comes from his *Gaozi, shang* (first part), 8; see: http://ctext.org/mengzi/gaozi-i.

[21] The *Nanjing* or *Classic of Difficult Issues* is one of the main ancient texts on Chinese Medicine. It was translated into English and annotated by Unschuld (1986).

[22] The quote is not an exact one, but it paraphrases the meaning of the first chapter of the *Nanjing.* See Unschuld (1986): p. 65.

[23] A *li* is a traditional unit of distance that was only standardized during the People's Republic. It was roughly about 400 meters in ancient times.

Earth is called "the Great Void". Within it is contained the One *Qi* of Former Heaven[24], which turns around endlessly. Laozi[25] says: "The shape of Heaven and Earth is like the nozzle of a bellows." At rest it closes and in motion it opens up. Man also resembles this, as Heaven and man are one, are they not? As for man, if one investigates thoroughly the time before one is born, before one possesses the Seven Emotions[26], when the Five *Skandhas*[27] are originally empty, then there is only One Round Illuminating Light

---

[24] The One *Qi* of Former Heaven refers to the united condition of qi before it divides into *Yinqi* and *Yangqi* and is then further subdivided. There are two Heavenly conditions: Former Heaven and Later Heaven. The two conditions can be represented by a different order of the Eight Trigrams or *Bagua*. Former Heaven stands for a more original condition. In man, for instance, it is the condition that is innate. During one's life it is gradually replaced by the condition of Later Heaven, which is seen as a deterioration of life and this ultimately leads to disintegration and death. In Taoist alchemy, the practitioner reinforces the Former Heavenly condition, restores the unity of qi (called "*Yuanqi*" or "Primary *Qi*" and also "*Yiqi*" or "One *Qi*"), and consolidates life by doing so. (S)he rejuvenates in this way.

[25] Laozi's *Daodejing*, chapter 5 mentions the bellows. See: http://ctext.org/dao-de-jing. In this chapter, however, the text reads not exactly the same, since the *Daodejing* says: "What is between Heaven and Earth, is it not like the bellows?" In internal alchemy, the bellows actually refers to the breathing. Several texts that are of interest to the alchemist refer to it. The movement of qi in between the head and the abdomen in the alchemist's body may be compared to the movement of qi between Heaven and Earth.

[26] In Chinese Medicine the emotions are divided into seven: anger, joy, thought/toil, grief, fear, concern/sorrow, and fright. All are related to function-regions (*zangfu*) and conduits of circulation in the body (*jingluo*). See Vercammen (1995): p. 176.

[27] The Five *Skandhas* (*wuyun*) or *Pañcaskandha* are seen by the Buddhists as the five accumulations (or aggregates or components) of a human being. They are: *se* or the physical form, *shou* or the functioning of the senses in relation to affairs/things, *xiang* or the distinguishing mind, *xing* or the mind's processes regarding such things as (dis)likes, and *shi* or the cognitive mind.

of Awareness.[28] If one then becomes aware of the place where this breathing movement arises and returns, one shall already know where the breathing movement resides. When *Shen*[29] and *Qi* then unite in one, they make the One *Qi* of Former Heaven. If indeed one does not know that the Mechanism[30] enters more when at rest and exits more when in motion, the Ancestral *Qi*[31] inside the body will necessarily be robbed by Heaven. When the robbing is complete, the bodily shape will then die. If you know this, you shall gather when in motion and nourish when at rest. The *Qi* of Heaven is also robbed by man. After a long time, one is full and then both bodily shape and *Shen* are wonderful. One lives as long as a *kalpa*.[32] Therefore, in case one is able to rob Heavenly *Qi*, one spontaneously becomes long-lived and long lasting. When man

---

[28] The One Round Illuminating Light of Awareness refers to the bright light that is seen by the practitioner during his/her practice, when a unified condition (the One) is reached by the merging of Yin and Yang, represented by the images of sun and moon (together creating the character "*ming*", which refers to illumination). Roundness is a sign of something complete in Chinese philosophy-religion. Therefore, the light's roundness symbolizes the completing of a stage of practice. Awareness is seen as awakening from a condition of being asleep, i.e. unaware. This passage in the text is very Buddhist in content.

[29] *Shen* is a refined condition of *Qi*, man's vital breath. In Taoist Alchemy, *Shen* is transformed from a substance that is more Yin to a substance that is purely Yang. This is done by merging it with *Qi*, which is basically Yang.

[30] The (Heavenly) Mechanism or (*Tian*)*ji* is the dynamic force that is present in man and the entire cosmos. It derives its function from the interaction of Yin and Yang. See Pregadio (2008): pp. 536-7.

[31] The Ancestral *Qi* is another name for the first One *Qi* of Former Heaven. See Hu Fuchen (1995): p. 1219.

[32] A *kalpa* is the period of time between the creation and recreation of a universe. The term has entered Chinese usage via Buddhism.

knows that one's own *Xin*[33] is the breathing movement, he can collect into the One *Qi* of Former Heaven the Three, namely *Jing*, *Qi* and *Shen*.[34] The authentic *Xian*[35] of the successive generations have all used *Shen* and *Qi* for mutual infusion and the stopping of both breathing and thoughts as their method. However, man in general does not know about this word: "breathing" (*xi*).[36] What he knows is nasal breathing. Accordingly, he may know the flow of nasal breathing and he may also be able to nourish the body itself. After a long time Authentic Breathing may also reveal itself internally. Authentic Breathing is not breathing in and out through the nose. It is actually what the *Zhuangzi* proclaims[37]:

---

[33] *Xin* is the ruler of the body. It is also the function-region (*zang*) in the upper and central areas of the body. The heart and brain belong to this function-region, but it is also involved in digestion, and in many other processes in the body. It is considered in Chinese Medicine to be the house of *Shen* or Spirit(ual *Qi*).

[34] The Three are the so-called Three Treasures or *Sanbao*: Essence (*Jing*), Vital Breath (*Qi*), and Spirit (*Shen*) in their united condition. They are the three ingredients of the internal alchemical recipe and the objects of refinement.

[35] *Xian* are usually interpreted as "Immortals". They are those practitioners of Taoism, and Taoist Alchemy in particular, that transcend the human condition and live "as long as Heaven and Earth". One of the characters used for "*Xian*" shows a combination of the character for man and that for mountain, meaning that it concerns mountain people (people who withdraw to and live in the mountains) and/or people that are as stable as a mountain. Another version of the character shows their transcendent nature (or their ability to "fly").

[36] A play of words: since "*xi*" means both "to stop" and "to breathe", the actual idea is that when one reaches the stage where breathing stops, the true breathing or Authentic Breathing appears. The nose and mouth cease to breathe and all breathing is done internally.

[37] See http://ctext.org/zhuangzi (chapter 6: "The Master of the Great Ancestry") or Burton Watson's translation of the *Zhuangzi*: http://terebess.hu/english/chuangtzu. html#6. Or its paper version: Watson (1968) on p. 78.

"The breathing of the Authentic Man works by means of the heels." Using the heels, each and every breath returns to the navel. Below it communicates with the Sea of Qi[38], above it penetrates the Capital of the Spirits.[39] And so it is the place where the body is produced and the location where the Medicine[40] is obtained and the Embryo[41] is formed. If man is not rooted in this, a suffering body[42] will manifest itself. When one daily follows false teachers and fabricated explanations, one will not only spend one's thoughts in vain, but also delude oneself and others. And in the end one will not know. Wouldn't that be pitiful?!

---

[38] The Sea of Qi is situated in the abdomen and may refer to the (Lower) Field of Cinnabar or (Xia) Dantian. It is the region where the practitioner gathers his/her qi in order to refine it.

[39] The Capital of the Spirits is situated in the upper regions of the body or in the (Upper) Field of Cinnabar or (Shang) Dantian.

[40] The Medicine is one of the names for (different) products produced in the body through the alchemical processes. It is thus named because it is supposed to cure the body of illness. In the times when experimental or external alchemy was popular, the product of the alchemical work was often ingested as a medicinal pill, hence the name, also in the internal versions of alchemy.

[41] Part of the practice of internal alchemy resembles a pregnancy. The practitioner develops an Immortal Embryo, that will be born as a Child when ready to leave the body. It is then to be nourished for some time, so that it can become a full-grown Authentic Person. Of course, this should not be taken too literally, although the process does create physical symptoms that make a comparison with pregnancy not so far-fetched.

[42] Yet another term that gives away its Buddhist origin (the first Buddhist Truth being that life is suffering). The author of the preface definitely was heavily influenced by Buddhism and Confucianism.

When I was young, I was as stupid and dull-witted as Ksudrapanthaka[43], remembering one gāthā.[44] In the end, I obtained the Previous and left behind the Later,[45] but I still kept saying: "What else?" Therefore, first Sima[46] only taught me in a shallow, superficial way the counting of breath, so that I could clean out my distracting thoughts. It was of help to silently gain knowledge. I carried it out obediently and really examined it, but was destined to not yet understand its utmost principle and there was no leisure to ask for further progress. Later, I studied the method of Stopping and Observing of Tiantai Buddhism[47] and further used the regulation of breath as a bridge. Each time I regulated my breath, my worldly troubles ceased and were cast away. And I rejoiced it even more in my heart. But, easily going

---

[43] This name comes from a Buddhist story about twin brothers, the youngest of which was called Ksudrapanthaka (Mean Path). His brother was the clever one, while he was so stupid that he could not even remember his own name. However, he did become a disciple of the Buddha.

[44] The Chinese sound *"jiatuo"* is used for the Sanskrit word *"gāthā"*, which is a stanza or verse.

[45] The road to follow in practice is to revert to a more original condition.

[46] Sima may be his teacher, but it is quite possible that he is referring to Sima Chengzhen, a Taoist Master (647-735) from the Tang Dynasty, who wrote several works on Taoist practice. See Kohn (1987).

[47] *Zhiguan* (or stopping and observing) is a practice used in Tiantai Buddhism. The stopping stands for the body at rest, whereas the observation refers to the mind seeing clearly. The monk Zhi Yi (538-597), founder of Tiantai Buddhism, explains this practice in his text *Mohe Zhiguan (The Great Stopping and Observing)*, a most fundamental text of Tiantai Buddhism. Tiantai is a mountainous region in what is now the province of Zhejiang, south of Shanghai. It is the origin of Tiantai Buddhism, but also of the Southern Tradition of Jindan (the Golden Cinnabar), the most influential Taoist alchemical tradition. Regarding Buddhist practice, *zhi* may be seen as "cessation" and *guan* as "insight meditation". See Kohn (1989): pp. 195-6.

with the flow, I couldn't avoid sudden rejection. Fortunately, I got a visit from alchemical master Bai Yunzhai[48] from Yecheng[49], who encouraged me to study with zeal. I consequently received his intentions and gradually made some progress. My alchemical master's *zi*-name is "Mingzhi"; he is also styled "Zaixuzi".[50] He was fond of practice, but did not dread the hardship along the way. He went looking for the *Dao* in the regions of Qi, Lu and Chu, and the five Springs and Autumns.[51] He met a *Xian* somewhere between

---

[For] an introduction to the Chinese Buddhist Tiantai and Chan traditions, see for instance Paul Swanson's text: https://web.archive.org/web/20070710064157/http://www.nanzan-u.ac.jp/~pswanson/mhck/Chih-i%20on%20Zen%20and%20Chih-kuan%208-2003.pdf.

[48] Bai Yunzhai originated from what is now Nanjing (in Jiangsu province) and lived at the end of the Ming period (17th century). He became known and gained influence as the compiler of an annotated index to the Taoist Canon (*Zhengtong Daozang*, published in 1445): the *Daozang Mulu Xiangzhu* or *Detailed Annotations on the Catalogue of the Taoist Canon* (1626). By the time this preface was written, Bai was long gone. However, it was common practice in Taoist circles during the Qing dynasty to engage in "planchette writing": a spirit would possess the writer, who by automatic writing would then produce texts inspired by the spirit of a deceased Taoist master (in this case Bai Yunzhai). Long before that time Taoist traditions were transmitted by revelations and meetings with past Taoist masters or Immortals. See, for instance, Michael Strickmann's *Le taoïsme du Mao Chan, chronique d'une révélation* (1981).

[49] Yecheng is the ancient name of Nanjing.

[50] Chinese people, especially if they are literati, use several names. They have a *xing*, comparable to a surname, a *ming* (personal name), a *zi* (courtesy name), and some *hao* (for instance, for Taoists this is a name that is decided upon by the teacher or the elders in a tradition; it is, in such a case, used to indicate a generation with one part [a character] of the *hao* being used by all disciples of the same generation). One can also choose one or more *hao* for oneself. The *hao* mentioned here means "the Master (or Child) Who Resides in the Void".

[51] These are all old names for regions of China, dating back to the so-called Chunqiu (Spring and Autumn) period (770 BCE-476 BCE). Qi and Lu are northern regions, whereas Chu is situated in the south and center of China.

Taoshan and Qinling[52], and received his instructions and indications. He returned to a cloud cave in Longquan[53] to test them. In Huayang Dongtian[54] he concealed himself and shut himself off from the world to practice the secret method that was taught to him. After a full three years, he felt fully harmonized and in complete abundance. He could take to the air, like a *luan*[55] or a crane taking off. Later on, he handed down his writings about the Three Teachings and the One Hundred Schools of Thought[56], in an orderly way connected to the sources, taking nourishment from the ancients and containing the modern. They contain nothing that is not rooted in this authentic method. He first examined it on himself and then issued explanation on its profound meaning, expecting to provide simple illumination and easy practice, that is all. Taking hold of ancient knowledge and having been proved in the present, the method must be orthodox. It does not use strange

---

[52] Taoshan may be a mountainous region in the province of Zhejiang or in the province of Anhui and Qinling is a mountain chain, mostly in Shanxi province.

[53] Longquan is situated in the province of Zhejiang near a mountain chain. It is a place that is famous for the production of swords. A cloud cave is a deep grotto in the high mountains.

[54] Huayang Dongtian is a mountain cave in the Mao mountains (Maoshan) in the province of Jiangsu, an ancient Taoist holy mountain region. A "*dongtian* (grotto-heaven)" is a dwelling place of the Immortals. See *Dongtian Shengjing/Famous Centres of Taoism* (1987): p. 10 for a picture of the Huayang Dongtian. More information about the Maoshan Taoists can be found in Strickmann (1981).

[55] A *luan* is a fabulous bird. It is usually considered to be the male of the *feng* (often interpreted as "phoenix").

[56] The Three Teachings are the main traditions of China: Confucianism, Taoism, and Buddhism. The One Hundred Schools of Thought refer to all the philosophies and religions of China.

wording, does not cheat the world, nor does it startle people. It actually provides a "fly-whip", if one wants to be free of snow falling heavily.[57] It holds compassion and universally helps people with a suffering heart.[58] For me, it honestly made me search out the essentials of the *Dao.* I cannot bear to keep it for myself and shall transmit it via my own writing: *Direct Instructions for the Five Breathings.*

I am touched by my alchemical master's kindness and I also obtained the Original Breathing, the Heel Breathing, the Embryonic Breathing, and the United Primary Breathing.[59] I took my leave and diligently practiced them in sequence. Finally, all of a sudden, I obtained the blended state of *Wuji.*[60] The wonder of *Taiji's* movement and tranquillity were before my eyes.[61] Would I ever

---

[57] The "fly-whip" is a traditional attribute (and weapon) of Buddhists and Taoists. One of the names for this whip is *fuchen* or dust sweeper and "dust" is a Buddhist metaphor for the worldly troubles caused by one's passions. It can therefore symbolize the removal of life's suffering.

[58] This sentence also betrays its Buddhist influence: compassion can help in removing people's suffering.

[59] All of these will be explained in the main text that follows.

[60] The word *Wuji* literally means "without a ridgepole" and is often used in combination with *Taiji*, which is the "great ridgepole". *Wuji* refers to boundlessness, without limits, whereas *Taiji* (see note 61) is the supreme limit of the cosmos. In Taoism, *Taiji* is seen as the One that comes from *Wuji* and thus *Wuji* is associated with *Dao*, since *Dao* produces the One (*Daodejing* chapter 42). Both the *Daodejing* (chapter 28) and the *Zhuangzi* (chapter 1) mention *Wuji* in a context that describes limitlessness. The author of this preface uses *Wuji* to describe the condition an alchemist may experience during the practice, when everything blends into one and nothing can be discriminated. See Pregadio (2008): pp. 1057-9 for a description of *Wuji* and *Taiji*.

[61] *Taiji* is the One that unites Yin and Yang. It is the Great Ultimate or Great Ridgepole. Being the One, it comes just before *Wuji* in the Taoist practice of returning to the roots.

leave the place where Heaven and man exchange and connect? I beseeched my teacher to make this public to all those who are likewise inclined, so that those who engage in the study would have single-mindedness and would not be deluded by side-doors[62], that they would share in the return to the region of the Great *Dao* and the manifest skill. How could a teacher treat this lightly?

The former is the original preface by Feiqing layman[63] Gu Zuanshao of Changsha.[64] The fifteenth day of the tenth lunar month, 1826.

Lingxuanzi, Wang Shaofu of Boyang edited the original preface again on the birthday of Doumu[65], the fifteenth day of the first lunar month in the fifth year of Guangxu (1879).

---

[62] It is customary to warn people for practices that sometimes use the same name(s) as the authentic thing, but lead astray. These practices are called "side-doors" or "oblique (meaning "crooked") paths". A Taoist is supposed to make crooked roads straight instead of following them.

[63] A Buddhist or Taoist who doesn't live in a monastery and (usually) has a wife and/or family is called a *jushi*, a person who lives in the middle of worldly troubles and temptations.

[64] Changsha is now the capital city of the province of Hunan.

[65] Doumu or the Mother of the Dipper is a deity (of Indian roots, corresponding to Marīci in Brahmanic mythology) in Taoist religion. She is supposed to chase away illness and bring prosperity. Some hold that she is formed out of the One *Qi* of Former Heaven.

Note to this preface:[66]

The discussion of the method of the Five Breathings feels close to Neo-Confucianism. Only the wording comes from miscellaneous sources of the Three Teachings: Confucianism, Buddhism and Taoism. As to the spirit of the text, it is somewhat alienated and seems not pure.

When one writes at the end: "Original preface by Gu Zuanshao of Changsha, 1826" and then writes again "Edited original preface by Wang Shaofu of Boyang in the fifth year of Guangxu", then it makes one doubtful, if one reviews it. If one says that this preface was composed by Gu and then one also has "original preface" under Wang's edit, that is like saying Wang composed it. But, under the original text there very clearly are the words "original preface" of Gu. When one examines ways of editing, then there has never been such an example. People in the old days only had editing of books and texts, I have never seen the case that original prefaces could be edited. Readers afterwards must also have had these doubts about this.

---

[66] The texts in italics here and below are the annotations made by Chang Zunxian.

Added Explanatory Preface

to the

Edited Explanation of the Obscurities

in the

Direct Instructions for the Five Breathings

People from China and abroad in the old days and in the present were/are constrained by the creative and transformative [forces] of Heaven and Earth. [That condition] is brought in motion by the Qi of Yinyang. In Heaven and Earth, this is the Gate of Heaven[67]; in people, it is expiration and inspiration. One expiration and one inspiration, this is called one breathing. This is the one Great Dao within Qian and Kun.[68] When I personally investigate this path, I don't go looking for a specific gateway and I make no distinction between religions. All writings that relate to this path must be sought out and verified. This writing is a trustworthy source - which I obtained from the valuable storage place of a friend - to divulge the actual purpose of our Yellow Emperor and the Taoists. I gave it to the owner of the Yihuatang[69], wishing to make this path more widely known. It delightfully responds to mister

---

[67] The Gate of Heaven is situated in the northwest.

[68] *Qian* and *Kun* are two trigrams. *Qian*, the Creative, is represented as three full lines, whereas *Kun*, the Receptive, is composed of three broken lines. *Qian* also stands for Heaven and *Kun* for Earth.

[69] The Yihuatang was the publishing house in Shanghai that published and circulated the writings of alchemist and scholar Chen Yingning and his alchemical circle. See Liu (2009): p. 19 a.o.

Zhang Zhuming's original purpose for the Yangshan [Magazine][70], [namely] by completing it. To make it attractive and honor it, I added annotations to it. In my view then, it is about the Embryonic Breathing [found] in the writings of all the masters. Being easy to comprehend and clear in meaning, it can function as a short-cut to the practice, a start for those who begin studying the Dao. Therefore, I am pleased to have made the added annotations to correct it, to complete the excellent thought and to establish a foundation for the Dao, by divulging the secrets of this text and establishing the stairs for the first steps. Although being about the utmost of the One Breathing, it is also sufficient to explain the wonderful apertures of Heaven and Earth's Yinyang in this case.

This is the preface.

Written as a preface by Chang Zunxian from Xiangyin[71] at the Study for Expanding the Dao in Shanghai in the year yihai according to the traditional cycle, in the second month of the twenty-fourth year of the Chinese Republic (1935).

---

[70] The *Yangshan Magazine* (*Yangshan Banyue Kan* or *Biweekly to Promote the Good*), of which Chang Zunxian was an editor, was used as an important means to promote the revival of alchemy by Chen Yingning and his entourage. The complete collection of this magazine's issues was republished in 2005 by Chen's disciple Hu Haiya. See Hu and Wu (2005).

[71] Xiangyin is situated in Hunan. See Liu (2009): pp. 182-191 for a profile of Chang Zunxian.

The Edited Explanation of the Obscurities

in the

Direct Instructions for the Five Breathings

with Added Annotations

Original Work by Zaixuzi, Bai Yunzhai of Yecheng

Editing by Wang (Yikuan) Shaofu, Lingxuanzi of Boyang

Added Annotations by Chang Zunxian, Fisherman
of the Xiao,

Tributary of the Xiang, of Xiangyin

Sitting

When you enter the room to sit, first use a thick cushion. Place a wooden [object shaped as a] *manshou* (tiny round bread) under the cushion to support the anus. You can pull up one or both legs. The left hand is placed on top of the right palm; put them under the navel. Straighten the trunk and sit upright. Stretch the lumbar vertebrae region. Ears and shoulders are in line. Nose and navel are in line. Close the lips and keep the tongue in. Drop the eyelids, while looking straight ahead. *Xin*'s Primary *Shen* (*Yuanshen*) leads *Yi*'s Authentic Thought[72], following the light of both eyes to

---

[72] In the body function-region *Xin* the *Shen* ("Spirit(s)") is stored. The Primary *Shen* refers to the united first condition of *Shen*, before it becomes split up and shattered by the life ordinary people lead. The Taoist Alchemist practices a way of reversal,

concentrate on the tip of the nose, then going to the *Qi* Cavity (*Qixue*) under the navel. Allow it to be spontaneous, as if it were idle. Practice the counting of breath.

Basically, the path of development and cultivation belongs to the techniques of protecting life.[73] *These originally come from the* Yellow Emperor's Internal Classic, *as in the* "Treatise on the Corresponding Images of *Yinyang*",[74] *where it says:* "Wise men practice Undoing (*Wuwei*)[75] *and take pleasure in the capacity of being tranquil. They follow their wish to cheerfully keep their mind bent on guarding Empty Nothingness* (Xuwu). *That is why their long life is limitless and they will end with Heaven and Earth. This is the wise man's governing of the body.*"

Now, the so-called guarding of Undoing, Tranquillity, and Empty Nothingness is actually the method of quiet sitting. Therefore, people who practice development and cultivation, must select an

---

of returning to the source, meaning that (s)he reverses the shattering, the division to return to unity. This united condition is called "*Yuan*" (Primary). Thought, represented by *Yi*'s Authentic Thought, is the intermediary between the action in the Field of Cinnabar (*Dantian*) in the abdomen (also the *Qi* Cavity or *Qixue*) and the action in the upper regions of the body where *Shen* belongs.

[73] The techniques of protecting life are manifold. There are health exercises, diets, meditation, and many other practices. These are seen as (part of) the origin of the Taoist path of development and cultivation.

[74] This fragment from chapter 5 is translated from the Chinese original text by myself. See *Huangdi Neijing Suwen Jiao Shi (shang)* (1995): p. 84 for the Chinese original text and Unschuld and Tessenow (2011): pp. 115-6 for another translation.

[75] The expression *Wuwei* has several layers of meaning: one is undoing, meaning to get rid of acquired knowledge and habits and the like, to revert to a spontaneous condition; another is not interfering when all is running as it should.

area where the air is peaceful, a room that is really clean and pure and do quiet sitting in there.

As to the method of placing a wooden manshou *to support the anus, this does not seem to be necessary. According to the Yellow Emperor's Internal Classic, the anus communicates with* dachang,[76] *and so it is a gateway for the entering and exiting of External Qi (Waiqi).[77] If the Internal Qi (Neiqi) rises to the Room of Shen (Shenshi)[78], it moves through both Qiao [vessels of the feet] and the Control, Function and other vessels,[79] and doesn't*

---

[76] *Dachang* is the Yang part of the dual function-region *fei-dachang*. This function-region governs a.o. the breathing and the lower actions of the digestive system. *Dachang* also includes the large intestine, which exits via the anus. Because of it being a part of the *fei-dachang* system, it is also concerned with breathing and it therefore plays an important part in breathing exercises. During the practice the practitioner may experience (External) *Qi* entering and leaving the anus (note: actual breathing is meant, not farting).

[77] External *Qi* is thus called, because it comes from and depends upon the outside of the body. Internal *Qi* is a product of the body's alchemical transformations and does not depend on the external.

[78] The Room of *Shen* ("Spirit") maybe a place between the *Shèn* (water region, in the lower back and abdomen) and *Xin* (fire region, in the chest and head) function-regions. Another explanation is that it is the Yellow Court (*Huangting*) in the center of the body, where the soil region is located (water, soil, and fire being three of the Five Agents or *Wuxing* in the ancient *Wuxing* theory; the other two Agents are wood and metal). In any case, it is a place where *Shen* ("Spirit") and *Qi* meet during the process of alchemical refining.

[79] There are Eight Alchemical Vessels or *Bamai* in the body, that open up only by alchemical transformations of the body and are hidden (nonfunctional) in ordinary people. The Control and Function Vessels are best known, but there exist six lesser known vessels. Their use is to make the transformation from an ordinary being into a *Xian* (Immortal) possible. See Vercammen (1995): p. 170 for a discussion of the *Mai*.

communicate with the anus. Because of this, the movement of the Primary Qi (Yuanqi)[80] could in no way leave from the anus.

As for dropping the eyelids and looking straight ahead, that means lowering the eyelids and looking internally at Xin and Shen. Lead the Authentic Thought inside Yi following both eyes to concentrate on the tip of the nose. Move gradually to the Qi Cavity under the navel. Allow the breathing of Qi to happen spontaneously. Xin and Shen are both tranquil; they do not hear and do not see; they are as if entering a state of unconsciousness or idleness. Then practice the method of counting the breathing to stir the spirit. This then is the initial method to follow the inspiration and expiration of External Qi.

---

[80] The Primary *Qi* is the united, original condition of the *Qi*. See Vercammen (2000): pp. 15-29 for an in-depth explanation of *Yuanqi*.

Ordinary Breathing

There are four nasal breathings: Wind, Panting, *Qi,* and Breathing (*Xi*). When breathing is noisy, it is called "Wind". When breathing is short and hurried, it is called "Panting". When the coming and going of the breathing is not subtle, it is called "*Qi*". When breathing is continuous, without interruption, it is called "Breathing (*Xi*)". In the case of Wind there is scattering; Panting is violent; *Qi* is tiring, and Breathing is stable. From these four only the stable one [can] gradually approach regulating [breath]. It nourishes the body. This is Ordinary Breathing.

In a piece of writing from the Simple Questions *Qi Bo says to the Yellow Emperor[81]: "One expiration and one inspiration of man, [that] is breathing. Expiration and inspiration constitute breathing; they interact with a great breathing. They are called: "common people"." That makes it so that one expiration and one inspiration make one breathing. If we now say "nasal breathing" (when we carry on from the quiet sitting in the text above) then, with lips closed and tongue stored, we therefore only have*

---

[81] The *Simple Questions* or *Suwen* is the first part of the *Internal Classic Text of the Yellow Emperor*, one of the fundamental texts of Chinese Medicine. Just like the second part, the *Numinous Axis* or *Lingshu*, it contains eighty-one chapters. The quote I translate here is based on chapter 18 (*Qi Phenomena in Common People*). It is, however, not a complete and not an exact quote. See Unschuld and Tessenow (2011): pp. 301-2 for another translation of the original correct and complete text.

Qi *breathing in the nose. To differentiate into four explanations (Wind, Panting,* Qi, *and Breathing) is also similar to [what is written in] the* "Treatise on Vital *Qi" in the* Internal Classic.[82] *Also, to take only the stable one from the four explanations as approaching regulating [breath], quite attains the aim of the Taoists to nourish the External* Qi *by regulating it.*

---

[82] Chapter 3 of the Simple Questions or *Suwen* (*Shengqi Tong Tian Lun* or *Treatise on Vital Qi Communicating with Heaven*). See Unschuld and Tessenow: pp. 59-81.

Observing Breathing

What is the use of observation in breathing? Well, man's mind easily creates thoughts and thinking enters all the time. This thinking has not yet been put to an end, when yet another thought again comes in. *Xin* and *Shen* become tired by excessive work. With each passing day, *Qi* is consumed and the body weakens. When the body dies, the *Shen* leaves and enters transmigration again. Isn't that pitiful?! When one restores the Authenticity, the purpose is to free [oneself] from this. One must first stop the thoughts. How are thoughts stopped? Without observation it is impossible. In ancient times, it was said that the Great *Dao* teaches people first to stop thinking. If thoughts do not cease, [all] is also in vain. So, this is a matter of life and death. The method is to follow with observation where thoughts go. When the thoughts are with the breathing, observation is with the breathing. When the thoughts follow the exiting and entering of the breathing, observation follows the exiting and entering of the breathing. When all thoughts depend on breathing, every breath must be observed. When observation is stable and does not shift, thoughts will then stop. After a long time all three [types] (Wind, Panting and *Qi*) will all be gone. You shall spontaneously obtain that *Shen* and *Qi* unite into one and return to the Root!

This is the method to refine thoughts at the start of the study. After the thoughts have thus been refined, you can practice the

Five Breathings. The method of the Five Breathings has its foundation in this.

According to the Shuowen *etymological dictionary[83], the analysis of "guan (observation)" is "watching attentively". Since you are watching attentively with the eyes, there must be something with a shape [to watch]. However, if you do nasal breathing, there is no shape you can watch. If we now say "observation" in this case, carrying on from what we said after the quiet sitting with closed eyes in the text above, [we actually mean that] man's* Shen *is connected with both eyes. When* Shen *is not concentrated, [the sight of] the eyes also do[es] not see. Because the eyes follow* Shen, Shen *follows Xin, Xin* follows Yi, *and Yi* follows the thoughts, *this method follows the exiting and entering of breath with thought. Xin, Shen, Yi, and eyes then all follow it. After doing this for a long time, breath and thought both follow the internal observation and become stable. They spontaneously unite into one and return to the Root. The method of Observing and Stopping of Tiantai [Buddhism] is maybe just this![84]*

---

[83] The *Shuowen* (or *Graphs Explained*) is an etymological dictionary of the Eastern Han period. Although published in 100, it is still being used today. The etymological explanations in this dictionary are heavily influenced by Confucianist thought. Taoists often analyze characters in a different way.

[84] The commentator refers to the *Zhiguan* (Stopping and Observing) method of Tiantai Buddhism. See note 47 above.

First Method: Counting Breath

Counting breath is preliminary training. That man is being led by things is an old sore. *Xin* leaves its place without you being able to do something. If you then force it, it becomes even more chaotic. When you use the thoughts (belonging to *Xin*) to concentrate on the method of breathing, you can tie down the thoughts so that they don't go off wandering chaotically. Start counting from when the breathing is rough until the breathing is subtle; that is when you stop. Starting out from one breath count till it is not chaotic anymore (after a hundred, a thousand or ten thousand breaths). Then breathing will spontaneously become subtle. If in the middle [of this process] another thought suddenly arises, then count again. Only when, after a hundred/a thousand/ten thousand breaths, you get to [the stage] when you do not let one thought arise, this *Xin* [does not] leave (s) its place.[85] Gradually becoming well versed, you then practice the skill of regulating breath. Although counting breath is an awkward method, it is the easiest one and the one with the least problems. It is not like the forced practice of closing off the breath [done] on high mountain tops, which gives one problems.[86] Ranking the counting of breath, it naturally is not up to the standard of all those shortcuts to the

---

[85] There is no negation in this sentence in the Chinese original, but this is clearly a mistake, as one can see from the preceding text.

[86] The character translated as "problems" is "*bing*", which fundamentally means "illness".

Secret Purpose, such as the Mother of Metal's Observing of *Xin*, Laozi's Observing of the Apertures, and Ancestor Lü's Jade Purity's Practice of Condensing *Shen* into the *Qi* Cavity.[87] But, counting breath really suits the first study.

When we examine the method of counting the breath, its most detailed [description] comes from Baopuzi's chapter "Clearing up the Stagnant".[88] *Its method goes like this: when you start studying the moving of* Qi, *draw* Qi *into the nose and close it off. Keeping it in the dark, count by means of* Xin *until one hundred and twenty and then exhale it gently through the mouth. Now, when drawing it, you never want your own ears to hear the sound of exiting or entering. Constantly let much enter and few exit. When it gradually turns by itself, increase the counting by* Xin. *After a long time you can do it a thousand times. When you reach a thousand, then you become young again, if you are old. It daily revolves, as*

---

[87] A list of names of Taoist practices. The Observing of *Xin* refers to internal visualization of one's purified heart. The Mother of Metal (Jinmu) is actually the Queen Mother of the West (Xiwangmu; see Pregadio [2008], pp. 1119-21), a very popular Taoist deity often seen as a savior. The method of Observing the Apertures, here ascribed to Laozi, is also an internal visualization practice where one observes the apertures through which the *Qi* enters and exits. Usually this refers to the "Aperture within the Aperture" (*Qiaozhong Qiao*) in the *Qi* Cavity (*Qixue*). Ancestor Lü is Lü Dongbin, who probably lived during the late Tang and/or early Song. Taoist master Lü is one of the Eight Immortals or *Baxian*. He is held in high esteem by Taoist alchemists who regard him as a patriarch. Jade Purity is the name of a Taoist Heaven and the Practice of Condensing *Shen* into the *Qi* Cavity is part of the alchemical training.

[88] *Baopuzi* (*The Master Who Embraces Simplicity*) is a text written by Ge Hong (284-344). It is also his Taoist name. This commentary is based on *Baopuzi*, chapter 8. See Ware (1966): pp. 138-140 for a translation of the practice of breath. For more detailed information about the book, read Pregadio (2008): pp. 215-7.

one says! Few [methods] are similar to this method. I especially recorded this to provide readers with the quotation for reference.

Second Method: Regulating Breath

Where counting and regulating differ is that counting uses *Yi*[89] to count, whereas regulating regulates without *Yi*. Only one thought focuses on breath and breath is actually [represented as] the tip of the nose. In the old days, it was said that to get it (coming) only depends on the tip of the nose. This is the first beginners' method of Observing and Stopping, for the main purpose of stopping thoughts and repulsing *Mo*.[90] After a long time, breath is regulated spontaneously. Having regulated until the skill is profound, you gradually approach Heel Breathing.[91] However, during the regulating of breath, one must constantly make it continuous and dense. It is as if it is hardly there. In this way, *Xin* is stabilized and

---

[89] One use of *Yi* is as one's focus or attention. *Yi* can also indicate consciousness and imagination.

[90] *Mo* are often interpreted as "demons". They are "*Qi*-creatures" that live inside the practitioner's body. They seem to enter from the outside, giving rise to the expression in Taoist alchemical circles of "*rumo*" (entering demons). In fact, they are caused by impurity of *Qi* inside one's body's *Xin*, the ruler of the body (mainly meaning one's thoughts and emotions). During the training each and every practitioner meets his/her *Mo*, once a certain level is reached (interaction between *Qi* and *Shen*). Because they delude the practitioner and appear to him/her as genuine, the practitioner is in real danger during this phase. If there is no knowledgeable teacher available when they first appear, the student can be in serious trouble. When practice is done in the proper way, and especially when the preparation has been done in the right way, they disappear again. They are cut to pieces by "the sword of *Yi*", meaning that, to get through this phase, focus and insight are of the utmost importance. When, through practice, the student purifies and yang-ifies his/her *Qi*, no trace is left of *Mo* and Authentic *Yi* (insight) appears. In my opinion, *rumo* is best interpreted as "entering (*ru*) the phase when hallucinations and illusions (*mo*) arise" instead of "entering demons".

[91] See below (Third Method) for an explanation of Heel Breathing.

Yi is at rest. *Shen* and *Qi* return to the Root. The Apertures of the Mechanism are gradually revealed. During the trancelike state there is no acquaintance, no knowledge. Body and *Xin* are still. You are only aware that breath and thoughts are interdependent and *Shen* and *Qi* unite with each other. When reaching [the level where] mouth and nose do little and the movements in the Field of Cinnabar are numerous, you come close to Heel Breathing. When you then practice Heel Breathing, you enter the Authenthic *Dao*!

The Inscription about Embryonic Breathing[92] *says: "Swallow thirty-six times. The first swallowing must be put first [i.e. breathe in and swallow saliva before expelling breath]. Expelling is only done very subtly, taking in only very softly. When sitting or lying down, it is also like this and when walking or standing, act calmly. Guard against noise and diversion, abstain from meat and fish smell. Also named "Embryonic Breathing"[93], it is actually called "Internal Cinnabar".[94] It not only treats illnesses, it decisively prolongs life. When you practice it for a very long time, your name will be listed among the higher* Xian." *Wang Wenlu from the Ming*

---

[92] This text is fully named the *Inscription about the Internal Cinnabar of the Embryonic Breathing (Taixi Neidan Ming)*. Its origin can be traced to the Tang (7th-10th century). The quote here is not exact, but very similar to the original. About the original see: Schipper and Verellen (2004): pp. 366-7. Different versions of the original appear in two important Taoist text collections: the *Taoist Canon (Daozang)* of the Ming and the *Seven Lots from the Bookbag of the Clouds* or *Yunji Qiqian* of the Song. See also notes 92 and 113 below.

[93] See below for a description of the Embryonic Breathing.

[94] Or Internal Alchemy; according to the text of the *Inscription* Embryonic Breathing is therefore Internal Alchemy.

Dynasty commented[95]*: "This is the* Inscription about Embryonic Breathing. *Regulate* Qi *and swallow [saliva] fluid to repair the Primary* Qi *of the Central Palace. Each double hour*[96] *swallow three times. When swallowing it at the* zi *double hour*[97]*, it particularly nourishes life." If you combine this method with the others, you may have some result.*

---

[95] This writer came from Jiaxing in what is now Zhejiang province. This quote comes from his *Commentaries of the Classic on Embryonic Breathing* (*Taixi Jing Shu*). See Fang (1989): p. 342.

[96] Traditionally the day and night were divided into twelve double hours or *shi*.

[97] The period from 11 pm to 1 am is the *zi* double hour.

Third Method: Heel Breathing

An ordinary man breathes by means of his throat, an Authentic Man breathes by means of his heels.[98] The heels reach deep to the *Qi* Cavity, and the *Qi* Cavity is the location of expiration and inspiration. It is also called the "Field Where Four Meet".[99] The *Classic of the Yellow Court*[100] says: "At the back you have the Secret Door; at the front the Gate of Production. Where the Sun comes out and the Moon enters expiration and inspiration exist." That is this. However, it is not so that the ordinary man does not [use] the heels, [but] his *Shen* is not contained within. Indulging its speeding outwards, he is not aware that he does it by means of his throat. The Authentic Man's thoughts constantly rely on breathing. His *Shen* enters the *Qi* Cavity. Indeed, it is constantly continuous and dense, existing without space in between. He can therefore concentrate his *Qi* to bring about softness, embracing oneness without leaving it. Void to the utmost and seriously at

---

[98] A quote from *Zhuangzi*; see footnote 37 above.

[99] Four of the eight extraordinary vessels meet there: the Control Vessel (*Dumai*), the Function Vessel (*Renmai*), the Belt Vessel (*Daimai*), and the Thoroughfare Vessel (*Chongmai*).

[100] The *Huangtingjing* or *Classic of the Yellow Court* is an ancient and most influential Taoist text, of which two main versions (a so-called "internal" and "external") exist. For a discussion of the text, see Schipper (1975). Information about its contents can be found in Pregadio (2008): pp. 511-4. It describes the interior of the body in a symbolic language that refers to the ancient Taoist view of the body as a landscape. This usage was picked up by later alchemists and expanded. This quote comes from the internal version, see Schipper (1975), p. 1**.

rest. Only then shall one observe its return. With the heel, one treads on the Aperture of the Void, and expiration and inspiration are to be found in this circle. When students focus the United *Yi* of the *Shen* Light in their eyes on the deep(est) location of breath, that is entering the *Qi* Cavity (the Aperture Within the Aperture). *Xin* will spontaneously become empty and quiet, while *Qi* will spontaneously fill up. After one hundred days the skill will be profound, and you will definitely have the intended result. The quieter the observation of *Xin*, the more complete the consolidation of *Shen* will be. The more stable the Authentic Breathing becomes, the more sufficient the Primary *Qi* will be. These [results] all come from the effect of consolidating *Shen* in the *Qi* Cavity. At the beginning of Heel Breathing, when *Shen* consolidates within *Qi*, focus on the location of expiration and inspiration and go down to the Cavity of *Qi*. When exhaling, it will descend and when inhaling, it will rise. We call it the "Revolving Circulating Heaven".

Note: "Heel Breathing" comes from the chapter The Master of the Great Ancestry *in Zhuangzi's* Classic from the South of China[101], *where it reads: "The breathing of the Authentic Man is done by means of the heels; the breathing of the masses is done by means of the throat." A* Jade Piece of Writing[102] *says: "The heel is the back of the foot." So, mister Hu Yuanru once said*

---

[101] The *Classic from the South of China* is the traditional Taoist designation of the *Zhuangzi* text. See footnote 37.

[102] A *Yupian* or *Jade Piece of Writing* refers to a text transmitted by the gods or spirits.

about Zhuangzi's comment in his writing, quoting master Chen Yingning's words[103]: "Breathing refers to internal expiration and inspiration. The heel refers to the Yinqiao *Vessel from the Eight Vessels of the Extraordinary Conduits, because this vessel rises below in the heel of the foot and runs upwards to the throat. Basically it branches off from the Shaoyin Conduit of the Foot[104] and can penetrate the Bubbling Spring cavity.[105] In the masses this vessel is constantly closed, but Authentic People make this pass burst open by means of Former Heaven Yangqi.[106] Therefore, they are able to let it penetrate upwards in the Heavenly Valley[107] in one expiration, and to let it reach the Bubbling Spring below in one inspiration. It revolves day and night, unceasingly. When the scriptures say: "Rubbing the crown of the head, loosen the*

---

[103] Chen Yingning (1880–1969) was the most important person in the recent history of Taoist alchemy. As a practitioner and a scholar he was ideally suited to publish and comment on the alchemical texts, which was exactly what he did, thereby saving them from "extinction". See Liu (2009) for a fine study of Chen and his alchemical circle. Hu Yuanru or Hu Yuanjun (1869-1933) was a scholar of Taoist philosophy and a close friend of Chen Yingning's father. More on Hu can be found in Liu (2009), pp. 44-5.

[104] The *Shaoyin* (Young *Yin*) Conduit of the Foot is the *Qi* circulation that connects with the *Shèn* function-region (*zang*) in the abdomen. In this function-region the Lower Field of Cinnabar can be found.

[105] The *Yongquan Xue* or Bubbling Spring Cavity belongs to the *Shaoyin* Conduit of the Foot and is situated in a central position on the sole of the foot. It is connected with the abdomen and some of the functions that are active in that region, a.o. the *Dantian* or Cinnabar Field.

[106] Former Heaven *Yangqi* is the refined *Qi* that forms the means to complete the alchemical process. The practitioner has returned his/her *Qi* from a Later Heaven condition to a more original condition.

[107] The Heavenly Valley is another name for the (Palace of) the Mud Pellet (*Niwan*[*gong*]). This Palace is also called the Upper Cinnabar Field (*Shang Dantian*).

heels", they are saying that from the crown of the head above it reaches down to the heels. When you check the ways of practicing of the Xian experts, the most important is that the Authentic Qi penetrates the Mud Pellet (Niwan)[108] above and reaches the Bubbling Spring (Yongquan) below." Master Yingning's words are profoundly in agreement with the Main Purpose[109], and, moreover, grasp the real meaning of the word "heel". They seem to hit the mark quite well. I especially recorded them to correct the mistake of the original explanation.

---

[108] The Mud Pellet or Mud Ball (*Niwan*) is situated in the brain; see the previous footnote.

[109] This Main Purpose is a synonym of the goal of Taoist internal alchemy.

Fourth Method: Embryonic Breathing

After practicing Heel Breathing for a long time, with *Yi*[110] becoming purer, breathing will become more subtle. The more *Shen* consolidates, the more *Qi* will be nourished. There shall be no breathing out and in through the nose, only a subtle breathing coming and going underneath the navel. It descends at the front and rises at the back. Like with a child in the womb, breathing returns to the navel. We call this "Embryonic Breathing". *Shen* and *Qi* are greatly stabilized, spontaneously being themselves. It is not to be compared with the forced shutting off and letting flow [as done] on high mountain tops. It consists in being able to let one thought condense inside, while *Shen* and breathing are interdependent. Common people are disordered all the time, their *Shen* and *Qi* become weary and tired. They are totally dependent on a good night's sleep, to even start to have enough for daily use. Otherwise, the originally pure *Qi* is covered by the impure. Moreover, hankering after food, they harm the spirit of life time and again, without regard for revenge for their wrongdoing and the payback later.[111] Also, consuming meat, fish, and alcohol easily sets licentious thoughts in motion. Entering the bedroom drunk, with a heart loving sexual desire, the *Jing* will leak and the *Qi* will

---

[110] In this chapter the most important "ingredients" of the practice reappear: *Yi* (Focus and Consciousness), *Jing* (Essence, the basic material), *Qi* (Vital Breath), and Shen (Spirit). See footnote 34 above.

[111] The author here follows the Buddhist concept of karma retribution.

be consumed. *Shen* will be wounded and life shortened. Every day getting closer to death, stupidly unaware.

Baopuzi says[112]: *"By letting the* Qi *move one can prolong life."* *What is greatly necessary is Embryonic Breathing, that is all. In case one gets Embryonic Breathing, one is able to breathe out and in through the nose and mouth*[113] *like inside the womb, and then* Dao *is completed! Why, this method also springs forth from Baopuzi!*

Regarding Authentic Men, they breathe without sleeping. They refine this *Shen* and *Qi*, and *Yi* becomes one without disorder. Their ears seem not to hear, although they do hear. Their eyes seem not to see, although they do see. Straightening the body, they sit upright. Their *Yi* only consolidates *Shen*, focusing on the location of expiration and inspiration. Breathing and thoughts are interdependent, *Shen* and *Qi* are joined together, exchanging in the Internal Apertures. They are like a hen brooding eggs, leaving the nest not for an instant. They also resemble live cinders, constantly in the furnace. The Authentic *Qi* becomes more sufficient every day, and the Primary *Shen* becomes more vigorous with the day. Curled up young male and female dragons, the two of them not separating from one another. When one gets to share one's body with the Empty Void, one shares one's lifespan with the Empty

---

[112] *Baopuzi*, chapter 6. See Ware (1966), p. 113 for a translation.

[113] Generally, Embryonic Breathing is considered to be breathing without the use of nose and mouth.

Void spontaneously. Stabilizing the breathing seven times seven, the Primary *Yangqi* is born. Stabilizing the breathing for a hundred days, the work on the Small Medicine is complete. Stabilizing breathing [after that] for seven days, the Great Medicine is already formed. Stabilizing breath for ten months, an Embryonic *Xian* will then be formed. Nurse it for three years, face the wall for nine years, and the exiting *Shen* will enter stability. By not abandoning the nourishing by means of warmth, not only will the leaking cease, but *Xing* will have the Six Penetrations. The body will display rosy clouds and the eyes will seem like the light of lightning. When entering the water, one does not drown and when entering fire, one does not burn. One's disappearing and appearing will be unfathomable, an Earthly *Shenxian*.[114] One will widely establish virtuous merits in order to affect all Heavens. One can expect transcendence and being lifted upwards, waiting to be made a Heavenly *Xian*.[115]

The Classic about Embryonic Breathing[116] *says: "The Embryo is formed out of concealed* Qi." *An explanatory note by mister*

---

[114] A *(Shen)xian* or (Spiritual) Immortal is the designation for someone who has reached a high level of practice and has transcended the ordinary human condition. Several "levels" or "ranks" of Immortals exist. An Earthly *Xian* is a lower rank than a Heavenly *Xian*.

[115] Heavenly Immortals can ascend to Heaven, riding a crane or mounting a cloud.

[116] The *Taixijing* or *Classic about Embryonic Breathing* is different from the *Taixi (Neidan) Ming* mentioned in footnote 92. Mister Huanzhen is the Taoist name of an unknown Taoist master from the Tang. Some see him not only as the commentator of the text, but also as its author: see Schipper and Verellen (2004), pp. 366-7 and

Huanzhen says: "One who practices Dao *constantly conceals his/ her* Qi *below the navel, and guards his/her* Shen *inside the body.* Shen *and* Qi *join together to produce the Dark Embryo. Since the Dark Embryo has then been formed, it spontaneously produces a body. And this is the Path of Immortality of* Neidan *(Internal Alchemy)." Wang Wenlu*[117] *of the Ming Dynasty said in a commentary: "Concealment initiates the forming of the Embryo. When the Embryo is formed, it will breathe. This originally started to show people that one shall concentrate* Qi *to bring about softness like a baby." Reading it suffices to prove the tenet of the meaning of this. One must study Yingningzi's* The Meaning of the Classic Text of the Yellow Court Explained *for reference, and then it will be even more easily understood.*[118]

Maspero (1971), p. 507. The text ascribed to Huanzhen is called *Commentary of the Classic about Embryonic Breathing (Taixijing Zhu)*. It can be found in the *Daozang* (130, fasc. 59) and in the *Yunji Qiqian* (1988 reprint, scroll 60, pp. 337-341 for Huanzhen's writings and p. 341 for the *Classic*). The text and annotations can also be found in Fang (1989), p. 341.

[117] Wang is already mentioned above in footnote 95.

[118] This refers to one of Chen Yingning's publications (Chinese title: *Huangtingjing Jiangyi*; originally published in 1933 by the Yihuatang, it was republished in the 1980s by the Chinese Taoist Association). See also Liu (2009) pp. 87-8 a.o.

Fifth Method: United Primary Breathing

Above we discussed the skill of stabilizing breath by Embryonic Breathing. When the stabilization of breath has been done for a long time, the Six Pulses[119] all stop. Hardly any *Qi* exits from mouth or nose. There is only a Void, communicating through the Heavenly Aperture.[120] With the Great Void united in one, there is full infusion between the both of them. One is only aware of a round light that covers Heaven and Earth. After a long time, one does not know [the difference between] things and oneself, [things with] form and [things that are] empty. Both words and thoughts are broken off, speech and silence are both forgotten. *Shen* hides in *Qi*, and *Qi* is embraced by *Shen*. The One *Yi* blends with harmony, wrapping up *Hundun*.[121] It is as if cinders continually [light] each other, keeping the caldron constantly warm. If one is able to refine for an instant, there is one instant of Circulating

---

[119] The Six Pulses refer to six fundamental types of pulse that can be experienced when feeling the pulse in Chinese medical diagnostics. According to chapter 4 of the *Classic of Difficult Issues* (*Nanjing*) the six are: floating, sunken, long, short, slippery and rough. See also Unschuld (1986), pp. 101-2 for a translation (but in the translation two types of pulse are omitted!). The meaning is that the ordinary human condition stops and a new type of (immortal) life is created.

[120] This Heavenly Aperture is located on the top of the skull. In alchemical practice the opening of the *sinciput* by the *Qi* creates an aperture through which the *Yangshen* can exit the body. This happens when the Embryo is ready to be born.

[121] *Hundun*, often translated as "Chaos", refers to the (not necessarily chaotic) blended condition where nothing is differentiated and all is one. After creating the One, the practitioner of internal alchemy may enter this condition. See also Pregadio (2008) for different interpretations of *Hundun*.

Heaven.[122] If one is able to refine for a double hour, there is a double hour of Circulating Heaven. If one is able to refine for a hundred days, it accumulates to form the Great Medicine.[123] If one is able to refine for ten months, then it forms an Embryonic *Xian*. If one is able to refine for three years, the *Yangshen*[124] exits and enters. Once it has been stabilized for nine years, it transcends and lifts up to the Heavenly *Xian*. When merit and virtue are complete, you can await summoning to rise upwards.

---

[122] Circulating Heaven or *Zhoutian* is the circulation that links up the *Dumai* (Control Vessel) in the back with the *Renmai* (Function Vessel) in the front of the body. Through this circulation *Qi* is transported from the *Dantian* in the abdomen to the *Niwan* region in the head and back down to the *Dantian*. It is an important part of the recycling and transformation process in Taoist Alchemy. There are in fact two Circulating Heavens, one so-called Smaller (*Dumai - Renmai*) and one Larger, which connects the Microcosm of the body with the Macrocosm outside. Different opinions about what they are exist and different traditions and practitioners may therefore provide quite different explanations, especially about the Larger Circulating Heaven. The word *Zhoutian* is frequently interpreted as "Heavenly Circulation", an interpretation this writer does not agree with. It actually depends on the creation of a Heavenly condition in the body by Yang-ification. This Heavenly condition is symbolized by a re-arrangement of the internal order of the body through circulation. It is the turning of the closed-off (*zhou* meaning [making] a circuit and a cycle [such as a returning period, e.g. a week]) internal Heaven that creates this and it is not a circulation that depends on (external) Heaven. The connection with the external creates a Larger Heaven, hence the name Larger Circulating Heaven, when this happens. From a linguistic point of view, Heavenly Circulation would be *Tianyun*, for that matter, not *Zhoutian*.

[123] Four types of Medicine are mentioned in Taoist alchemical texts: the External, the Smaller, the Internal and the Larger or Great Medicine. They refer to different things or conditions. The Great Medicine is the combination of the External (coming from the external Macrocosm) and the Internal (produced in the body of the practitioner), when both congeal in the Lower Field of Cinnabar.

[124] Once the *Shen* is purified and refined to the utmost it is called *Yangshen*, because it is done by Yang-ification of the Shen, using internal "fire" (different ways of using Focus/Consciousness or *Yi*). The periods of time mentioned here are symbolical. Because the creation and development is seen as the development of an embryo, the phases resemble pregnancy (ten months), lactation (three years) and growing up to become a full-grown Authentic Person (*Zhenren*) or Immortal (*Xian*) (nine years).

Baopuzi says[125]*: "Every time one takes in Primary Qi, it does not follow the exiting and entering of the coarse Qi." Because the coarse Qi resides in the belly, it does not live together with the Primary Qi. If one looks after and protects the Primary Qi, one can remove illness. If one takes in Primary Qi, one can prolong life. If one consolidates Shen and makes Jing firm, and unites it by transformation with Primary Qi, then Shen hides in the Qi Cavity. After a long time, one's own and the Qi of Qian and Kun's Yinyang*[126] *communicate with each other. Then [one possesses] the skill to*

---

[125] This quote comes from the appendix to the *Inner Chapters of the Master Who Embraces Simplicity* or *Baopuzi Neipian*, a chapter called "Other Purposes" or "Bie Zhi". In Ware's translation (1966), this chapter is omitted. The original text can be found in the *Taoist Canon* or *Daozang* (CT 1185, fasc. 868-870) and in the *Complete Writings of All Masters (Baizi Quan Shu)*, a text collection containing many Chinese ancient philosophical writings, volume 8, p. 19a of scroll 4. On the *Baopuzi Neipian* see Schipper and Verellen (2004), pp. 70-1.

[126] *Qian* and *Kun* are two most important trigrams (and hexagrams, the symbols consisting of [un]broken lines from the *Yijing*), representing respectively Heaven and Earth. The Taoist alchemical practice consists of uniting the Cosmic Heaven and Earth with one's body Heaven and Earth. This is done by means of two "qualities" of *Qi*, namely *Yangqi* and *Yinqi*. The two *Qi* are represented in the trigrams by full (Yang) and broken (Yin) lines. The alchemical process can be represented by the interaction of these lines. The best known process is the exchange of the central lines of the trigrams *Kan* (symbolizing Water, in the northern position, the trigram with a broken or Yin line above and below the central unbroken or Yang line) and *Li* (symbolizing Fire, in the southern position, the trigram with an broken line between two unbroken ones) in the Later Heaven order of the practitioner's body, a process through which the practitioner's body reverts to the Former Heaven condition. In this Former Heaven condition, *Qian* (the trigram consisting of three Yang lines) then occupies the southern position, whereas *Kun* (the trigram consisting of three Yin lines) takes the northern position. For a description of the processes see Pregadio's translation of Wang Mu's book on internal alchemy (Wang [2011]), especially pages 126-8 for a visual representation. The use of trigrams to symbolize internal transformations in the alchemist's body became common practice after it was first introduced in the *Seal of the Unity of the Three (Zhouyi Cantongqi)*. For this book, see also Pregadio's translation: Pregadio (2011a & b).

advance and retire of the Fire Phases of the Circulating Heaven[127] *and the wonder of transforming the* Qi *into* Shen *by means of refining it. All this comes from this United Primary One* Qi, *that uses* Shen *[to achieve] its wonderful applications. When the skill is completed, it must be possible to rise up flying!*

All of this is breath's making a beginning and ending. Heaven and Earth exchange with each other without separating from this breath. The primary meeting that makes generations revolve, does not separate from this breath. Winter, spring, summer, and fall do not separate from this breath. Dawn, daytime, dusk, and night do not separate from this breath. One should know that this breath is suitable for Counting and Regulating, for Heel Breathing and stabilizing, up to [making it] United Primary [*Qi*] in the end. An instant's work [equals] a year's division. How much more is a double hour's, a day's, a month's, and a year's [work]?! Each time when you have the transformation of the United Primary [*Qi*] by the Circulating Heaven and you want to steal the Primary *Qi* of Heaven and Earth, you [must] first stabilize this breath. If you want to obtain the Authentic Mechanism of Creative Transformation,

---

[127] Internal Alchemy borrows images and terminology from Experimental or External Alchemy (*Waidan*). In the External Alchemy the production of the Medicine was done by means of fire, which had to be controlled, i.e. sometimes one needed a powerful fire (*Wuhuo* or Martial Fire) and sometimes a less powerful one (*Wenhuo* or Civil Fire). In the internal practice the interfering of the practitioner with the process, through use of *Xin* (the psycho-emotional faculties of the body), represented by *Yi* (Focus and Consciousness) and *Shen* ("Spirit"), must also follow suit. The use of *Xin* should be heavy in certain phases and non-existent in others; this is called advancing and retiring.

first seize this breath. But man is daily lost by bad habits, and is ignorant about Counting and Regulating Breath. Now, about the wonders of Heel Breathing, Embryonic Breathing, and United Primary Breathing, man throughout the world has even more difficulties to know. Well, a day and night of Heaven and Earth are thirteen thousand five hundred breaths [long]. A person in [the condition of] ordinary breathing does not know that man breathes out and in along with Heaven and Earth. How would he/she know about Authentic Breathing?!

Wunengzi[128] *says: "When Heaven and Earth are not yet distinguished, [there is] the United Primary One Qi. (...) When Heaven and Earth then take their positions, the Qi of Yin and Yang exchange." Man along with [other] things floats amidst Heaven and Earth and the One Qi comes to an end. Breathing is the expiration and inspiration of Qi. Primary Breathing is what is inside of expiration and inspiration. Moving internally, it can steal the transformative Qi of the United Primary [condition] of Heaven and Earth. Moving externally, it is not able to grasp the Authentic Mechanism of the Creative Transformation of Heaven and Earth.*

---

[128] *Wunengzi* or *The Master of No Abilities* is the title of a Taoist text from the Tang (probably 9th century). Its authorship is shrouded in mystery. This quote is not exact and incomplete, but is based on the beginning of the *Wunengzi* (chapter 1: "The Mistakes of the Holy Men" or "Sheng Guo"). *Wunengzi* is part of the Taoist Canon (CT 1028) and there is a critical edition by Wang Ming (1981). I have used the *Complete Writings of All Masters* (*Baizi Quan Shu*) edition, where it appears in volume 8, on the first page (p. 1a) of the first scroll. It was translated into English by Woolley in 1997 (unpublished) and into Dutch by Jan de Meyer (2011), who shares his thoughts about who the *Wunengzi*'s author may have been on pp. 31-7. His Dutch translation of this quote can be found on p. 53.

Only Xian *experts show the ability to do the work in an instant. They can inhale the Authentic* Qi *of the four seasons of ancient and modern times in Heaven and on Earth in the time period of one breathing! If you wish to become well versed in this principle, you can, through reading, make yourself familiar with the preface to the* Four Hundred Characters about the Golden Cinnabar *by the Authentic Man Zhang Ziyang.*[129] *Then you shall obtain it.*

To sum up, people are moulded and cast by *Yinyang*. They are limited by the amount of *Qi*, get their retribution from causes and effects, and their lifespans are not equal. Although one may dodge the retribution for karma, one day the downfall will come.[130] This can be sad. A Person Who Has Arrived[131] fears retribution given by Heaven, and does not dare to recklessly do the slightest evil, knowing that when *Qi* fills up, *Shen* complies and one lives. He/she understands that with *Qi* consumed, *Shen* leaves and one dies. One ought to know that as long as one breath remains, *Xing* and *Ming* are still able to govern themselves. If one is able to practice the Five Breathings, one escapes from the Three Ways.[132]

---

[129] The *Four Hundred Characters about the Golden Cinnabar* or *Jindan Sibaizi* is one of the fundamental texts of the Southern Tradition of Taoist Alchemy. It is ascribed to Zhang Boduan (984/987-1082). See Vercammen (2003) for an annotated English translation of this text and the biographies of Zhang.

[130] The author is referring to Buddhist views again.

[131] A "Person Who Has Arrived" or *Zhiren* is one of the denominations of an accomplished Taoist master.

[132] The Three Ways meant here are three possible roads that can be followed after one dies. Because the successful practitioner of Taoist alchemy becomes an Immortal, (s)he escapes from this fate.

Sure enough, after two or three years of hardship, one shall definitely be happy for ten million *kalpas*. When the transformation of *Yinjing*[133] has come to an end and it has been refined into *Yangshen*, one reverts to the Root and returns to the Origin. One then forms a Holy Body, that takes shape when condensed and [appears as] a golden light when dispersed.[134] When one lets it go, it penetrates the Ten Extremes.[135] When one accumulates it, it hides in the point of a needle. One is within a foot from Penglai[136] and an instant away from the Golden Gate.[137] The Method of the Highest Vehicle[138] is nothing more than the Five Breathings. Why

---

[133] Ordinary *Jing* or Essence belongs to *Houtian* or Later Heaven, a condition that is present in ordinary people, who are far removed and moving further away from their original united condition. *Jing* is by nature a fluid and therefore belongs to Yin. The Alchemist reverts to the Origin, goes back to the Former Heaven condition and uses transformation in two fundamental steps to refine *Yinjing* into *Yangshen*: (s)he first refines *Jing* (Essence) into *Qi* (Refined Vital Breath), and then refines *Qi* into *Shen* (Subtle *Qi*-Spirit); *Shen* is then further refined until Nothing is left, whence it has returned to the Void.

[134] The Buddhist and Taoist views assume that the Holy Body, consisting of *Yangshen*, can condense and take shape or disperse, which may be seen as an explosion of light.

[135] The Ten Extremes are the eight cardinal directions and the zenith and nadir. It is more common in Buddhism than in Taoism to mention the Ten Directions. Taoists usually prefer the Eight Directions or *Bagua* (associated with the Eight Trigrams) and the Nine Palaces or *Jiugong* (eight directions/trigrams and the center).

[136] Penglai is the name used for the region where the Immortals live. It is usually referred to as islands in the ocean to the East of China.

[137] The Golden Gate is normally the Central Field of Cinnabar (*Zhong Dantian*), located in the chest, between the nipples, but here it refers to the Realm of the Immortals.

[138] This Method of the Highest Vehicle refers to Buddhism's Mahāyāna school.

use the Nine Reverting Motions[139], if only this is able to show results? One's shape and *Shen* will both be wonderful. To join in Authenticity with *Dao*, that is this.

Guai'aizi in Zhiyouzi's Piece on the Authentic Declarations[140] *says: "When I am guarding the One Clear* Qi, *I cannot let it contend with the Creative Transformations." People's lifespans are limited by the amount of* Qi, *yet, they all let them[141] drop themselves. In the case of a Person Who Has Arrived, (s)he refines the Authentic* Qi *of the Three Primaries[142], makes the Numinous Light of the Five Zang[143] coagulate, makes his/her breathing tranquil and consol-*

---

[139] The Nine Reverting Motions (*Jiuhuan*) or the Nine Turning Motions (*Jiuzhuan*) refer to the actual practice of Taoist (External) Alchemy, because reverting and turning upside down (symbolically done nine times) of the vessel that contained the ingredients to make the Elixir, was an important method in its preparation. The terminology is also used in Internal Alchemy.

[140] The *Zhengao* or *Authentic Declarations* (*Daozang* 1016, fasc. 637-640) was written by the influential Taoist master Tao Hongjing (456-536), the founder of the Shangqing (Highest Purity) Tradition of Taoism. Zhiyouzi or the Master Who Wanders Extremely is the Taoist name of Zeng Zao (12th century), a Southern Song scholar-official. Zhiyouzi's compilation of Taoist texts, the *Daoshu* or *Pivot of the Way*, contains the *Piece on the Authentic Declarations* (Zeng [1990], pp. 57-62). For a description of the contents of the *Daoshu*, see Pregadio (2008), pp. 329-331. However, this quote does not come from the *Piece on the Authentic Declarations*, but from the next text, namely the *Piece on the Yellow Court*! See Zeng (1990), p. 66. Guai'aizi is the sobriquet of Zhang Zhongding (946-1015), a mandarin and poet during the Northern Song.

[141] I.e. the amounts of *Qi* available.

[142] The Three Primaries or *Sanyuan* refer to Primary Essence (*Yuanjing*), Primary Breath (*Yuanqi*), and Primary Spirit (*Yuanshen*): the united, first conditions of the *Jing*, *Qi* and *Shen* (see also footnote 34).

[143] The Numinous Light of the Five Storage Places (Function-Regions) or *Zang* is their *Shenqi* or Spirit-*Qi*. The *Zang* light up when the ordinary *Qi* from food and beverages

idates the Shen. *And then the Embryo is nourished and the* Qi *is transformed. After three years, there is completion and after nine years, it transcends and is lifted upwards. There is nothing that is not completed by gradual progress of these Five Breathings!*

Note: the book on the method of the Five Breathings is also initial work for Taoists. It seems to stem from the Tradition of the Authentic Man Qiu Changchun of the Northern Seven Authentic [Persons].[144] *It can be of assistance to start out. This causes one to say: "The Method of the Highest Vehicle is nothing more than the Five Breathings. Why use the Nine Reverting Motions, if only this is able to show results?" Clearly this is self-contradictory with what is said in the previous part: in one hundred days it refines the Medicine, in ten months it forms the Embryo, after three years it enters stabilization, and after nine years it lets the* Shen *out. I therefore say that its wording and the tone of the text is not pure. So, the explanatory note gives a tool, because, if beginning students are without an initial method, they shall have trouble every time. By means of this, I provide them with guidance.*

---

has been expelled.

[144] Qiu Changchun or Qiu Chuji (1148-1227) was one of the disciples of Wang Chongyang (1112-1170) and an important figure in the development of Taoism in the North of China during the Yuan period (1279-1368). He is traditionally seen as the founder of the Longmen (Dragon Gate) Tradition of Quanzhen (Complete Authenticity) Taoism, although, according to Esposito, this is a myth (in Pregadio [2008], pp. 704-706). As to the Seven Authentic Persons (all disciples of Wang Chongyang), one can read the translation by Eva Wong (1990) of a Chinese novel about them.

Original Breathing[145]

Sitting is no empty sitting. Count the breathing, Regulate it, do Heel Breathing and Embryonic Breathing until you get to United Primary Breathing. One's own *Xin* is breathing (*xi*). Breathing and thoughts rely on one another and that is it. Its secret formula follows from both eyes looking at the *Qi* Cavity behind the navel. After a long time, thoughts return to one. When *Xin* is at its most tranquil state, Heel Breathing will then reveal itself. This bypasses the Counting of breath and the Regulation of breath and directly makes a start with Heel Breathing. If you do not obtain the secret of observing breath, you shall only know the counting of breath to stop distracting thoughts. If you practice Embryonic Breathing and [by doing this] you are without Wind or Panting [breath], it shall only belong to the expiration and inspiration of Later Heaven. It shall not happen apart from mouth and nose, and it shall not be Authentic expiration and inspiration. As for observing Heel Breathing, it is rooted deeply in the *Qi* Cavity. When you observe Embryonic Breathing, it moves in the Central Palace. Observing the United Primary Breathing, it is one with Heaven. These three breathings are therefore breathings of Authentic People. In the

---

[145] The three breathings mentioned above (Heel, Embryonic, and United Primary) develop out of the active practices of Counting and Regulating breath. There is, however an alternative way that leaves Counting and Regulating out. This is done by observing one's *Xin*, until spontaneously a deeper breathing arises. This practice is spontaneity to the extreme, a pure *Wuwei* (Undoing/Not Interfering) method. The author calls this "Original Breathing". It was this practice I studied first in China in 1985.

case of Counting breathing and Regulating breathing, they are expirations and inspirations with a form, and so they are the exiting and entering through mouth and nose of Later Heaven. They can only nourish the body. Heel Breathing, Embryonic Breathing, and United Primary Breathing, [they] issue from ancient writings that few can read, so they are definitely difficult to know by everyone in general.

So, this is the path of the Confucianists to stop, stabilize, and make quiet and peaceful, and [it is] the mechanism of the Buddhists of Observing and Stopping in order to understand the Void. However, the original principles all come from the writings of the philosophers. They have quite some research value!

People's life has *Qi* as its origin, *Shen* (Spirit) as its substance, *Yi* as its application, *Xin* as its root, and *Shèn* (the function-region in the abdomen and lower back) as its stem. *Xin* and *Shèn* are eight *cun*[146] and four *fen* apart. In the middle there is a vessel, that is the Thoroughfare Vessel. In the front there is a vessel that is called Function Vessel, and in the back there is one called the Overseeing Vessel.[147] In the middle between fore and aft at the top is a general

---

[146] A *cun* is a traditional unit of length, measuring the width of a thumb at the joint. A *fen* is the tenth part of it.

[147] Or the Control Vessel, located in the back.

assembly place, that is the Moon Cave, i.e. the Palace of *Wu*.[148]

In the middle between fore and aft below is a general gathering place, that is the Root of Heaven, i.e. the Palace of *Zi*.[149] The Heel Breathing comes from the Thoroughfare Vessel. Ordinary expiration and inspiration rely on the external. They require making the exiting and entering gradually more subtle. Authentic expiration and inspiration rely on the internal. They require that tranquillity is gradually stabilized. It is like a human in the womb, where breathing originates in the navel. When reaching [the time when] (s)he exits from the mother's belly, the breathing returns to the Three Fields.[150] Knowledge gradually opens up, and the desire for things gradually [starts] polluting. The Three Fields and the Vessels withdraw, and one tumbles into Later Heaven. There is breathing of *Qi* with form, and then it exits and enters through nose and mouth. Few people of the world know the root and origin

---

[148] The Moon Cave (*Yueku*) or the Palace of *Wu* (*Wugong*) is also called the Palace of the Mud Pellet (*Niwangong*) and the Upper Field of Cinnabar (*Shang Dantian*). *Zi* and *Wu* are the first and the seventh of the so-called Earthly Branches (*Dizhi*), characters that were traditionally used to designate time and space (in the outside world, as used, for instance, in *fengshui* geomancy, but also in the internal world or the Taoist description of the body). *Zi* can be associated with the North and 11 pm to 1 am, whereas *Wu* stands for the South and 11 am to 1 pm. In the human body the North is in the lower part of the trunk and the South is in the head. See Wang (2011), p. 131 for a list of the Earthly Branches.

[149] Below in the water region of the body or *Shèn* (the *Zang* or storage place in the lower back and abdomen that controls the kidneys, bladder, sexual organs, etc.) one finds the Root of Heaven (*Tiangen*) or Palace of *Zi* (*Zigong*). More information on the storage places can be found in Vercammen (1995), pp. 164-6.

[150] Three Cinnabar Fields are mentioned in some Taoist alchemical texts and traditions: one in the abdomen (the Lower Field), one in the chest (the Middle) and one in the head (the Upper Field).

of Heel Breathing. If you have the intention to seek knowledge, you shall wish to connect with *Dao*'s Destiny.

These principles mostly come from the Internal Classic of the Yellow Emperor *and they are also an important purpose of the arts of nourishing life. People who practice cannot but be acquainted [with it].*

If you want to understand the Authentic Mechanism of Heel Breathing, the extent of the work, and the true tranquillity, you must know that the Thoroughfare Vessel is the True Vessel of the Central Palace. It penetrates upwards into the root of the Mountains[151], up to the summit of the Kun[lun Mountains]. Downwards it penetrates in the navel, up to the Cavity of *Qi*. In the center there is a corresponding Valley, i.e. the Bellows[152], in between the back of the navel and the front of *Shèn*.[153] In the old days, they called it the *Yinyang* Aperture, the Gate of *Wu-Ji*[154], the

---

[151] The mountains refer to the skull bones. The top of the skull is named the Kunlun Mountains after the Kunlun mountains in the Northwest of China. In ancient times its location was not known exactly and it played a role in Chinese mythology.

[152] For the Bellows, see footnote 25 above.

[153] This *Shèn* is not the *Shen* ("Spirit"), but one of the function-regions of the body, based in the lower back and abdominal region and responsible for, a.o., the urinary and reproductive systems. The Lower *Dantian* belongs to this region.

[154] *Wu-Ji* refers to the Heavenly Stems (linked to the Earthly Branches system explained in footnote 148). *Wu* is the fifth of the Stems and *Ji* is the sixth one. These two Stems are associated with the center and soil in the system of the Five Agents

Crossroads, the Field Where Four Come Together, the Place Where the Body Is Produced, the Pass of the Renewal of Life, the Cave of Empty Nothingness, the Flute Without Holes, the Gate of the Dark Female, the Location of Expiration and Inspiration, the Palace of the Life of Wisdom, the Cave of Longevity, the Internal Dark Pass, the Cavity of *Shen-Qi*.[155] Although there are many different names, they are all this location.[156] Above the Thoroughfare Vessel is the External Dark Pass.[157] The middle of the Thoroughfare Vessel bears the name Central Dark Pass. Below the Thoroughfare Vessel is the Internal Dark Pass. This is by which the Principle exists, by which desire departs, *Yang* enters, and *Yin* retires. Bursting open when one exhales and closing when one inhales, where *Shen* comes together and *Qi* gathers, it really is an important pass. Now, as soon as breath is exhaled, all vessels altogether burst open, and as soon as breath is inhaled, all vessels altogether close.

(*Wuxing*: Wood, Fire, Soil, Metal, Water) and with all things that can be associated with the Agent Soil, such as the color yellow, the function-region *Pi* (responsible for the first part of the digestive system and located in the stomach region in the center of the body). See Wang (2011), p. 131, for the complete list of the Stems and Vercammen (1995), pp. 167-8, for an explanation of the *Wuxing* and a list of their associations. P. 125 in Wang also presents a table of the Agents and their associations.

[155] Different encoded names were often used for the same thing or region in Taoist literature. The names make it clear that this is a place of exchange.

[156] This paraphrases the first chapter of the *Daodejing* where it reads: "They exit identically, yet bear different names."

[157] The Dark (or Mysterious) Pass is sort of an alchemical secret, yet it is one of the most important experiences of the practice, because it marks the practitioner's passing from the Later Heaven condition to the Former Heaven one. What it is exactly is explained in different ways in different alchemical traditions. Because it has no form, it is in any case hard to describe. This text refers to three Dark Passes, one External, one Central and one Internal, and gives them a location. This is unusual.

When they burst open, *Yang* expands, and when they close, *Yin* accumulates. Bursting open is Dark, closing is Female.[158] Between one bursting open and one closing, that is the Dark Pass. When wind is generated by the closing and opening, that is also called the Bellows. It follows spontaneity and is also called the Wind of *Xun*.[159] The origin of expiration is the Sea of *Xing*, and inspiration returns to the Stem of *Ming*.[160] The *[Classic Text of] Southern China*, the *Zhuangzi*, also calls it Heel Breathing. The formula says: "When expiration and inspiration reach the Root and Stem, longevity can then be hoped for."

---

[158] This explains another alchemical secret, the so-called Dark (or Mysterious) Female or *Xuanpin*. The term comes from the *Daodejing*, chapter 6, where it is associated with other enigmatic terminology, such as the Spirit of the Valley and the Root of Heaven and Earth. Several explanations of its location and functions exist. See Pregadio (2008), pp. 1138-9, for an analysis and a drawing. In the practice, it is linked to the experience of opening (a Yang phenomenon) and closing (a Yin phenomenon) in the body of the practitioner, caused by transformations of *Qi* or Vital Breath.

[159] The trigram *Xun* symbolizes the wind and wind is associated with the breathing.

[160] *Xing* and *Ming* are the objects of restoration and development (called "*xiu*" in Chinese). *Xing* is often translated as "(Innate/Inner) Nature" and *Ming* as "Life" or "Vital Force". The two are intrinsically interconnected. *Ming* is associated with the lower back, where the so-called Gate of Life (*Mingmen*) is situated. Here man's life force and creative and reproductive capacities are located. Its expression is the *Qi* or Vital Breath. Because it stores certain intellectual capacities, it connects with *Xin* (the function-region that rules the body), and it is in fact the power that makes *Xin*'s working possible. *Xing* is often seen as located in *Xin*, yet, because *Xing* is also associated with sexuality, it is therefore also connected with the *Ming* region. In Taoist Internal Alchemy, most practitioners strive to revitalize the body by developing and refining the *Qi* (called *Ming* Practice or *Minggong*) and by restoring the original capacities of the body by reducing the impact of emotions and diminishing the troubles and vexations caused by thought (*Xing* Practice or *Xinggong*). Different traditions take different approaches to and maintain different views on how to proceed. See Pregadio (2008), pp. 1103-5. For an elaborate discussion in Chinese of the view on *xing* and *ming* in the Southern Tradition of Internal Alchemy, see Vercammen (2008). Also read Hu Fuchen's text on internal alchemy in Vercammen (2000), especially p. 33.

The meaning of this section corresponds with the principles of the methods in each and every classical text on alchemy. It also connects with the Illustration of the Closing and Bursting Open of Qian and Kun *by Shao Kangjie.*[161] *This [way of] discussing [this matter] is also seldom obtained.*

When one exhales, *Qi* hankers after *Shen*; it rises from the back and descends in the front [of the body]. In the center, it rouses itself. When one inhales, *Shen* hankers after *Qi;* it descends from the front and rises in the back. In the center, it enters by itself. The mechanism of rousing and entering resembles the Bellows of

---

[161] Shao Kangjie or Shao Yong (1011-1077) was an influential philosopher and poet during the Northern Song Dynasty. He wrote about the cosmology and the images and numbers of the *Yijing* and was influenced by the Northern Song Taoist Chen Tuan (871-989). This Chen Tuan is supposed to have made a drawing of the *Wuji*, which inspired the Neo-Confucianists to philosophize and write about *Wuji* and *Taiji* (see footnotes 60 and 61 above on *Wuji* and *Taiji*). In his book *The August Ultimate through the Ages* (*Huang Ji Jing Shi*; included in the *Daozang* as CT 1040) he discusses symbolic chronology (see Schipper and Verellen [2004], pp. 752-3). Although Shao was, of course, an eminent specialist of the hexagrams and trigrams of the *Yijing*, his book does not contain the illustration mentioned here. The illustration does appear in another book: see http://www.ctcwri.idv.tw/CT-DSXJ/CTDSXJ11太極周易卦理系列/易說/易說ALL/21乾坤闔闢圖解.pdf for an image and the text explaining it in the *Explanation of the Book (of Yinyang) Changes* by Master Lü (*Lüzi Yi Shuo*). Master Lü is Lü Yan or Lü Dongbin (known as a Taoist alchemist, poet, writer, sword-fighter, healer, etc.), who may have lived during the Tang and early Song dynasties. He is a semilegendary figure and several books are ascribed to him, though probably none of these texts were written by him. Most date from later times. The image can also be found in the *Records Transmitted from the Heart of Evidence Narrated in Detail* (*Xin Chuan Shu Zheng Lu*), which is part of the *Collected Essentials of the Taoist Canon* (*Daozang Jiyao*), an important collection of Taoist texts, the current edition of which dates from 1906. This book contains a preface written in 1803 by a certain Meifang Laoren (Old Man Plum Fragrance) from Suiyang (in what is now Henan province). See *Chongkan Daozang Jiyao*, section *Gui Ji* (*Gui* Collection) 7, p. 19, which shows the *Illustration of the Closing and Bursting Open of* Qian *and* Kun). On Shao Yong see Pregadio (2008), pp. 876-7; on Chen Tuan, pp. 257-9; on Lü Yan, pp. 712-4.

Heaven and Earth. The Bellows is the exiting and entering when exhaling and inhaling. It is the Mechanism by means of which Heaven and Man steal from each other. When it moves while you exhale, more exits; when it is at rest while you inhale, more enters. The mechanism of expiration and inspiration not only [involves] the responding to each other of the upper and lower [parts] in the center, but also the counter-revolving, fore and aft, relentlessly. It is like the never-ending revolving of a water wheel.

When one studies this and obtains the secrets of the observation of breath, then one shall know the alternating motion of the Central Palace, which is the foremost place to set out to work. If you do not meet the right person, you cannot teach it [to anyone] recklessly. Those who [are about to] know must first cultivate Virtue. If they do not amass good deeds, and practice recklessly, they will meet with reprimands. Tremble at this! Be cautious!

This section continues from the above in order to fully explain the meaning of expiration and inspiration. The so-called hankering after Qi *and* Shen *is in fact the aim of the* Xian *experts to make* Qi *and* Shen *join. Therefore, as soon as rousing and entering happen, you can communicate with the Bellows Mechanism of Heaven and Earth. This really makes one see the words of the* Dao!162

---

162 The original text and my translation end here. It is customary to end a text on such practices with a warning ("Tremble at this! Be cautious!"). Because of the occurrence of strange phenomena (the *rumo* phase, when hallucinations arise, for instance) these warnings are not out of place. Furthermore, words of warning were also used to protect the text's secrets, because they could prevent abuse of the practices by people with the wrong intentions.

Taoist Breathing Exercises

An Introduction to the Practice

by Dan KJ Vercammen

After reading the original text don't feel silly if you cannot really grasp what it is actually telling you. The amount of footnotes I had to put in makes it clear that the author of the text was supposing that the reader would have a good knowledge of Buddhism, Taoism, and Confucianism and their practices and texts. One cannot expect this kind of knowledge from the ordinary Chinese and non-Chinese person. The commentator tried to explain some of the backgrounds, but being well versed in Taoist and other literature and being taught by Chen Yingning, his writings also do not make things much clearer. It takes several readings of the original text to come to understand a bit more and it needs practice to link what you read with the experience of practicing Taoist (and other) breathing techniques. Therefore, I want to present you with a short introduction to the practices mentioned in the text. If you want to fully experience what is described in the *Direct Instructions for the Five Breathings*, a good guide (a Taoist Internal Alchemy master) is essential. This guide can help you practice safely and explain what is symbolic and what is actual practical information.

In fact, two main types of Taoist breathing techniques exist. They can be practiced one next to the other or one can practice just one type. The usual way is to start from techniques that prolong the duration of breath and that concentrate one's attention. After some time one can then move on to more spontaneous development of breath. The Chinese text translated in this book describes the stages of this spontaneous evolution. In Taoist terminology one moves from *Youwei* (active participation) to *Wuwei* (passive, spontaneous development and observation) when following this path.

It is necessary to understand that, although Taoist breathing exercises seem simple, they are actually far-reaching and can have complex results and lead to complications. Therefore, I would like to stress that, when practicing, it is important to take precautions and to stick to safe pathways, as described below. To experiment with mixed techniques and systems may cause problems and permanent damage to your health. Do not take this lightly; be warned! My predecessors and myself have taught these techniques in a certain way to prevent errors and problems, thus creating the right conditions for good and healthy results.

Taoist practice should not be used to advance oneself. Instead, one should try not to advance oneself in order to be advanced, as is mentioned in Laozi's *Daodejing* (the *Classic Text on the Way and Its Emanation [or Inner Power]*), one of Taoism's most fundamental texts.[163] This is the first and most important precaution. Forget about using your practice for fame, wealth and power, three common human goals that are better left behind, as the other fundamental Taoist text *Zhuangzi*, tells us.[164] Put your ego aside. Only by doing this will you be able to reach the highest levels. Other precautions that you should take are easier to achieve. They mainly concern the practical conditions of the practice. If they are not clear when reading through them, use common sense to remove doubt.

The practice consists of three distinct phases and each phase requires specific conditions.

---

[163] See *Daodejing*, chapters 7 and 66. See for Arthur Waley's English translation of the *Daodejing*: http://terebess.hu/english/tao/waley.html. The *Daodejing* is a very difficult text to translate, because it contains a lot of hidden information, i.e. one needs to experience Taoist practices and understand classical Chinese philosophy to be able to grasp some of its meaning. Also for Chinese it is difficult to understand the text. Many Chinese commentaries (providing explanations on the many dark passages) exist, showing that also for Chinese experts the text required explanation.

[164] A complete translation of the *Zhuangzi* was made by Burton Watson. The translation can be found on the internet: http://terebess.hu/english/chuangtzu.html. For instance, in chapter 28, Zhuangzi mentions the common human goals.

First Phase: Preparation

Preparation is a necessary first phase. Before doing the actual practice, you need to prepare yourself properly. Bad preparation leads to problems and/or lack of success. These conditions must be met:

practice should preferably be done inside a room and not outside in the open air; this room must be quiet, warm, dry (but not too dry) and free from draught

- practice should be done when you are not busy or occupied with all sorts of things or matters; traditionally, practice is therefore mostly done during the late evening, when natures invites you to take a rest; early morning after waking up when your thoughts are quiet is also a good time

- make sure nothing or nobody can disturb your practice; do not practice on an empty (unless you are combining it with fasting or a Taoist diet) or a full stomach (the digestive actions of your body will interfere with the movement and transformation of qi); do not practice when you are in urgent need to go to the toilet; resolve other "needs" that you may have first, so that they won't interfere with your practice; ask people to respect your private time

- position: Taoist breathing can be done while standing, sitting or lying down; each position has special requirements.

a. Standing Position

Several postures are possible; here we shall describe one of the main standing postures of *Yuanqigong* (the Practice of the Primary Breath), which is the practicing system we use: the *Wuji* (the Ultimateless) posture; stand with your feet shoulder-width apart, feet parallel to one another with the toes pointing slightly inwards; bend the legs a little and "sit", i. e. your sacrum should be perpendicular to the floor, naturally elongating your lower backbone while keeping the chest and belly relaxed; make your neck longer by positioning your ears above your shoulders and tuck your chin in just a little to make the curve of the neck almost disappear, thereby also elongating the middle region of your back; you should feel your back being stretched from your buttocks up to the crown of your head; relax your feet, make sure that the pressure from your body weight is transferred to those places on your feet where you have little "cushions": the heels, the outer edges, the toes and the cushions below the toes; shift more weight onto the front half of your feet, so that the *Yongquan* (Bubbling Spring)[165] cavity gets more pressure; avoid pressure on the inner edges of the feet (i. e. where the hollows are); relax shoulders and arms; keep the armpits open: do not press your upper arms against your body; make your arms as long as possible without stretching them; hold your hands in front of your *Dantian* (Field of

---

[165] This cavity can be found on the sole of the foot, in a central position in the hollow, in line with the middle toe.

Cinnabar, below the navel in the abdomen) with the palms facing the body; open your hands, keep the fingers relaxed but long, so that you feel a little stretching in your hands; your nose should be in a vertical line with your navel; it may take a while before you find the right position (a teacher can help you find it faster), but having found the right position, you will experience that it takes no effort to stand comfortably, even for longer periods of time, because you feel naturally supported or even "suspended between Heaven and Earth"; close your eyes; you are now ready to do the breathing exercises.[166]

---

[166] You can also hold the hands in front of the *Dantian* with the wrists bent and the palms facing the floor and the hands turned so that the little fingers are in front of the others. That requires more flexibility in the wrists and is therefore not recommended if by bending the wrists you feel tension in the hands and/or forearms.

b. Lying Down

Although it is possible to do breathing exercises while lying on the back it is preferable to practice while lying on the side; do not lay yourself down on the floor, use a bed or a sofa; the floor is the coldest part of a room (unless you have floor heating) and in a very relaxed condition the cold may enter your body more rapidly and more deeply than usual; avoid this! Support your head with a pillow, making sure that your backbone is as horizontal as possible when lying on your side; the leg that is on top should be long (without stretching it), the leg on which you are lying should be bent, with the foot touching the back of the knee of the other leg; in this way there is a little pressure on the *Weizhong* (the Soft Center)[167] cavity; beginners can put the arm below bent in front of the head with the palm of the hand facing upwards; the arm that is on top can be put on the thigh of the top leg with the palm of the hand on the thigh; elongate the backbone (similar to the standing position); close the eyes and start doing the breathing exercises.

---

[167] Located in the center of the back of the knee.

c. Sitting Position

You can sit on a chair, on a cushion, on your bed or on any other suitable, stable object; it is better not to sit on the floor; so, it is best to sit on a couch or bed if not sitting on a chair; the positions described below are the most suitable and advisable for beginners; it is preferable to sit in a relaxed way with hands open; therefore, sitting in a (half or full) lotus position is not recommended: it can be used in some practices, but is detrimental to your health by blocking blood circulation and damaging the joints of your legs, if you practice this frequently and for an extended period! At least during the first few weeks of the practice closing the hands is also not healthy, because one of the first things that happens when you are improving your breathing technique, is more circulation of the body's waste material towards the extremities; if you close your hands and diminish circulation in your legs, this waste material won't be able to exit fully and may remain inside the body; moreover, because of the increasing heat inside the trunk, it will start to move along with this heat to the top of the head, causing nausea and headache on the way; whether you sit on a chair or on something else, the body should be erect, meaning that the backbone should be as long as possible (similar to the standing position) and that the sacrum should be at a straight angle with the horizontal object you are sitting on; make sure your chest and belly are relaxed but not over-relaxed (don't collapse); put your hands on your knees with the palms facing upwards, hands open, fingers long; if you are sitting on a chair, put your feet shoulder-width apart, parallel to one another (see the standing position); the angle of your knees should be a little bit larger than 90°; if you sit on a bed or the like, bend your legs but do not cross them firmly, so that circulation is not hampered; do not lean against the wall or the back of a chair: your back should be free of external pressure; as briefly mentioned in the translated Chinese text, when sitting, you can put a (half) round object underneath your anus (to prevent hemorrhoids when sitting for extended periods); we usually shape a handkerchief into a ball and place this underneath the anus (do not use this handkerchief afterwards or before to blow your nose or wipe your sweat!); it should not be too soft nor too hard.

General Remarks For All Positions

Close your eyes and mouth; relax the tongue so that the tip touches the palate; make sure that your nose and navel line up vertically and that your ears and shoulders line up (when seen from the side); loosen long hair (do not tie it up), remove belt, wristwatch, glasses, lenses and other things that close off, press or diminish circulation; breathe slowly before proceeding; try to forget your daily chores and troubles.

Second Phase: the Beginning of Taoist Breathing Practice, its Conditions and Techniques

It is important that you realize that you are entering a new world and a special reality; you need to be guided in this new surrounding so that you do not get lost; do not regard this lightly, but stick to the guidelines and actions below!

a. The Beacons: after closing your eyes, focus on the tip of your nose, experience breath moving in and out through the nostrils while breathing slowly; then, focus on the navel and experience its movement as you breathe in and out; next, focus on the *Dantian*, i. e. the abdomen; then, start the breathing technique.

b. During the Practice: follow the instructions closely, nothing more and nothing less; changing the technique does not necessarily (and in most cases won't) produce the same effects; your aims should be regulation of breath, relaxation, circulation, and activation of the *Dantian*; never force your breath! As bad as they may be, follow the rhythm and capacities of your own breathing: they are yours and by using your own means your personal breathing can start evolving; breathe softly, do not add muscular contraction or expansion; sit straight if sitting, do not drop your position and recover your original position if you're sinking, bending or collapsing; <u>never</u> hold your breath, unless it is part of the technique; after some time during the practice, the *Dantian* will become activated and you can feel its agitation; this will cause spontaneous movements: the torso starts moving forwards and backwards a little, the torso starts to make circular movements, in the *Dantian* you may experience warmth, contractions, and so on; all of these are natural and normal reactions; do not oppose them, but let them happen; when standing, these movements can actually get quite big and numerous; it is advisable to seek guidance from a knowledgeable teacher in this case; when you feel you are heating up during the practice there are also a few things to consider: the heating up should start from the *Dantian* region and spread throughout the entire body; in case the head is becoming too warm or you start to feel nausea, your position is wrong; your backbone is not elongated enough or too tense, your stomach gets too much pressure, and your neck is not long enough or the muscles are too tight; also check if your chest is relaxed and whether your abdomen can move freely.

c. The End of the Practice Session: before ending the practice, focus again on the navel and breathe naturally and slowly; rub the forehead, the face, the chest and then the belly and abdomen a few times with a slight pressure; do this at least three times; then close your eyes firmly and open them widely three times; if sitting, wait a little before standing and moving; whatever your position, shake your body and especially your limbs a few times after the practice; stretch the backbone; move slowly and go easy for a few moments, before taking on other activities; drink some warm tea (or water) after the practice; never drink cold drinks or alcohol before or after the practice!

d. General Remarks about the Practice: although it is not the purpose, it can happen that you fall asleep while practicing; this is very common if you do the practice while lying down, but it can also happen while sitting (and in some rare cases even when standing); if you are lying in your bed and fall asleep, do not worry, you should actually sleep more firmly; if you fall asleep while sitting and you become aware of it, it is better to wake yourself up and finish the practice in the usual way, because otherwise you may end up sitting in an awkward position for a long time and this may cause muscular pain and the like; if thoughts arise during the practice, focus on the *Dantian* again and concentrate on the movement of breath or on your breathing technique to dispel the thoughts; thoughts are your enemies during the practice; you should get rid of them as soon as possible; focus and concentration are your friends.

Breathing Techniques

We shall discuss three types of techniques: fundamental (concentration exercises), regulating (prolonging and controlling breath),
and spontaneous techniques. Fundamental techniques can
produce regulating effects and can give rise to spontaneous
breathing changes. Regulating techniques feel less natural until
you reach the stage where your body starts doing them without
you actually inducing them consciously, and then they, too, create
spontaneous actions. Spontaneous techniques can easily lead to
distractions and aberrations, but in the end are what it is all about.
But, to be on the safe side, do not start with these spontaneous
practices first and seek out an experienced and careful teacher to
teach you how to proceed with them.

a. Fundamental Techniques

While these fundamental techniques are actual breathing exercises, they also serve the important purpose of helping to focus
and concentrate. Thye are called "*ruding*" or "entering stability
(a concentrated condition)". Staying focused and concentrated
is crucial, because this makes it possible to get rid of thoughts.
Thoughts interfere with and disturb natural breathing and it is only
when you are devoid of thoughts, that spontaneous breathing

appears and that the way you breathe is changed completely.[168] Take your time to integrate these fundamental techniques.

a. 1. Counting Breath

Counting your breathing is mentioned in the translated text as one of the initial techniques. It is popular in some Buddhist traditions as well as in Taoist ones. It is fairly easy to do. However, keep in mind that thoughts will try to interfere with your practice. If they do, start counting again and do so each time you get lost in thoughts. Do not worry about having thoughts. After all, that is only normal, but it is also natural to be able to disperse them and be free of thought. It just takes practice and time to get there. Be patient!

To start counting your breath, prepare yourself as described above. All breathing is done by means of the nose. One full breathing movement (inhaling and exhaling) is counted as one breath. Count every breath to maintain your focus and concentration. When you reach the stage where there are no thoughts and you don't count anymore, do not start counting again, because forgetting everything is your purpose. Only start counting again, if you forget to

---

[168] This spontaneous breathing is not the ordinary "natural" breathing. Instead, it is a developed breathing, created by intensive practice. It appears when thoughts cease to exist and focus, body, and breath are in perfect unified co-operation. This breathing is soft, deep and far-reaching.

count because of thoughts. To close the exercise, use the closing techniques described above.

For some people, counting the breath doesn't work well. If that is the case with you, then you can try the next technique instead. It is actually a little more advanced and is mentioned in the ancient Taoist text *Zhuangzi*.[169]

a. 2. Listening to Your Breath or Following Your Breath

Starting and closing the exercise is done as described above. Once you start the actual practice, you focus on the movement of your breath. Follow it, feel it, experience it, listen to it, while breathing in. Do not lose it. Do the same while breathing out. Keep going along with the breath. Do not focus on a specific spot or area, just keep following your breath. Do not get "stuck" with breath: if you feel that there are places where breathing doesn't seem to be able to pass, do not focus on them. Instead, remain with the movement, because, even if it seems as if breath stops in some places, it actually keeps moving. Do not worry if your breathing movements are very short. This will change with practice. If you are distracted by thoughts, focus on the movements of your breath again. If you reach the stage when you start forgetting everything, including following your breath, you are doing fine. It is only when

---

[169] This technique is described in chapter 4 of the *Zhuangzi*, see: http://terebess.hu/english/chuangtzu.html.

thoughts arise that you should start focusing again. All breathing is done by means of the nose.

In case this technique doesn't work for you, try counting your breath.

b. Regulating Techniques

We introduce two regulating techniques here. One is actually called regulating breath, the other is called closing off breath. These techniques aim at prolonging breath, i.e. they make breath go deeper and slower. In this way they prepare the body for more natural, spontaneous prolonging of breath, but, because these types of breath are induced and do not arise spontaneously, they do not last long after finishing the practice. Yet, it is useful to practice them.

b. 1. Regulating breath

Prepare as usual. This technique uses the nose to breathe in and the mouth (!) to breathe out. When using the mouth to breathe out, open it just a little, enough to let breath escape slowly. Breathe in until you cannot breathe in any further and you spontaneously start breathing out. Do this until you cannot breathe out anymore and you spontaneously start breathing in again. As a regular part of combined practice, this technique is done seven or nine times, but you can do more if you like. In combination with other breathing techniques, you can do this before doing the counting of or listening to breath. When you feel your breath getting restless while doing closing off (next technique), you can revert to regulating breath to stabilize your breath before continuing with the closing off. End the practice of this technique as usual, unless you continue with other techniques.

b. 2. Closing Off Breath

This technique is better not done at the beginning of your training. After some weeks or even months of practicing regulating breath, you can take up this challenge. It is recommended in the Southern Tradition of Taoist Alchemy (Jindan Nanzong) as a useful supporting practice for alchemical purposes. Prepare as usual, then regulate your breath seven times. Next, breathe in through the nose as with regulating breath. When breathing in is completed, stop breathing and hold your breath until you cannot hold it anymore; then breathe out. If possible, breathe out through the nose as slowly and tranquil as possible. If not possible, use the mouth as in regulating breath. Repeat for as long as possible. Do not overdo this. If you want to practice in a healthy way, start with a few times and add some each day. In case breathing gets rapid and you feel uncomfortable, practice regulating breath till breathing is stabilized again. It is also possible to close off breath after exhaling, meaning that you then do this routine: breathe in - close off - breathe out - close off. The duration of each segment of the practice will increase and it will have some influence on your usual breathing. End the practice as usual.

Third Phase: Spontaneous Techniques

Spontaneous breathing techniques belong to the *Wuwei* (undo-ing/not interfering) level of practice. You cannot interfere with what is happening to you and have to let things take their own turn. Because lots of things can happen during this practice, from a lot of movements to a lot of emotional changes, it is a practice that needs careful preparation and guidance. All too often in New Age and *qigong* circles, spontaneous action is (correctly) consid-ered to be very powerful, but underestimated as far as its possi-ble negative effects are concerned. Moreover, many so-called *qigong* masters feel the need to manipulate what happens to their students. Quite often their main goals are to show off their "exceptional skill" and to gain power over people. Frequently, they lack professional responsibility and medical skills, mean-ing that they may be able to induce more movements, etc. when their students are practicing spontaneous breathing, but they are unable to guide them as quickly as possible to the main goal of tranquility. Instead, they keep their students deliberately in the lower stage of spontaneous movements. This is interesting to the teacher, because then (s)he can still manipulate the students. Once a student reaches the tranquility levels, (s)he has created a condition that is difficult to manipulate from the outside. It will then look as if the teacher has "lost" his/her power. In fact, it is just then that the teacher shows his/her worth: (s)he has brought the student to a high level of practice.

Spontaneous techniques may still require the same preparation, posture(s) and positions, and the same ending techniques, until the student produces stability and is out of the "danger zone". Once you are focused and prepared, there is nothing more to do than to "sit and forget" (or stand/lie and forget, for that matter).

If you wish to practice this kind of technique you can get in touch with this author about how to practice in an efficient and, foremost, safe way.

The Use of Taoist Breathing

Taoist breathing is mainly used for improving health, inducing tranquility, and as a vehicle for creating subtle changes in the human body and mind, which can lead to more profound goals, such as those created by the practice of Taoist Alchemy. Some of these goals are described in the translated Chinese text. There are, however, also other uses. In Taoist medical practices, the practitioner often uses breath or *Qi* to communicate with the body of the patient. The same *Qi* is used in Taoist martial arts to help in developing the so-called Internal Energy (*Neijin*). This energy can be applied externally to destabilize and even hurt an adversary. These applications are not the subject of this book, though, which is why we cannot go into detail here. Some of this author's books do contain information about *Neijin* and the medical use of *Qi* (see bibliography), and future publications shall elaborate on these subjects.

Bibliography

Chinese Bibliography

Text collections and anonymous texts or texts with uncertainty about authorship are listed alphabetically on basis of their titles; other books are listed alphabetically on basis of their author(s).

百子全書 *Baizi Quanshu/The Complete Writings of All Philosophers* (1985 reprint in 8 volumes of 1919 reprint), Hangzhou: Zhejiang Renmin Chubanshe

陈撄宁 Chen, Yingning (reprint from the 1980s of a 1933 Yihuatang original), 黄庭经讲义 *Huangtingjing Jiangyi/The Meaning of the Classic Text of the Yellow Court Explained*, Zhongguo Daojiao Xiehui

辞海 *Cihai/Sea of Words* (1979), Shanghai: Shanghai Cishu Chubanshe

道藏 *Daozang/Taoist Canon* (1996 reprint in 36 volumes), Shanghai: Shanghai Shudian

方春陽 Fang, Chunyang (general editor) (1990²), 中國氣功大成 *Zhongguo Qigong Dacheng/Great Achievements of Chinese Qigong*, Jilin Kexue Jishu Chubanshe

費丹凝 Fei, Danning (Vercammen, Dan) (2008), 關於《先命後性》的幾個問題 *Guanyu "Xian Ming Hou Xing" de jige wenti/Some Issues about "First* Xing, *then* Ming*"*, Antwerp: China Arts

Bibliography

高鶴亭 Gao, Heting (general editor) (1991), 中華古典氣功文庫 *Zhonghua Gudian Qigong Wenku/The Chinese Library of Ancient Volumes on Qigong (14 volumes)*, Beijing: Beijing Chubanshe

郭靄春 Guo, Aichun (general editor) (2000), 黄帝内径词典 *Huangdi Neijing Cidian/Dictionary on the The Yellow Emperor's Internal Classic*, Tianjin: Tianjin Kexue Jishu Chubanshe

河北医学院 Hebei Yixueyuan/Medical Academy of Hebei (1984), 灵枢经校释 *Lingshujing Jiao Shi/Revision and Translation of the Spiritual Axis (2 volumes)*, Beijing: Renmin Weisheng Chubanshe

胡孚琛 Hu, Fuchen (general editor) (1995), 中华道教大辞典 *Zhonghua Daojiao Da Cidian/Big Dictionary of Chinese Taoism*, Beijing: Zhongguo Shehui Kexue Chubanshe

胡海牙, 武國忠 Hu, Haiya and Wu, Guozhong (2005), 揚善半月刊仙道月報全集 *Yangshan Banyue Kan, Xiandao Yuebao Quanji/Complete Collection of the Biweekly to Promote the Good and the Monthly of the Way of the Immortals (9 volumes)*, Beijing: Quanguo Tushuguan Suowei Fuzhi Zhongxin

闵智亭, 李养正 Min, Zhiting and Li, Yangzheng (general editors) (1994), 道教大辞典 *Daojiao Da Cidian/Big Dictionary of Taoism*, Beijing: Huaxia Chubanshe

Bibliography

山东中医学院，河北医学院 Shandong Zhongyi Xueyuan/Academy of Chinese Medicine of Shandong and Hebei Yixueyuan/Medical Academy of Hebei (1995[5]), 黄帝内经素问校释 *Huangdi Neijing Suwen Jiao Shi/Revision and Translation of the Simple Questions in the Yellow Emperor's Internal Classic (2 volumes)*, Beijing: Renmin Weisheng Chubanshe

邵雍 Shao, Yong (1993 revised edition of Ming original edition with commentaries by Huang Ji), 黃極經世 *Huangji Jing Shi/The August Ultimate through the Ages*, Zhengzhou: Zhongzhou Guji Chubanshe

沈洪训 Shen, Hongxun (private publication), 天山五息功 *Tianshan Wuxigong/Five Breathings Practice of the Heavenly Mountains* (small booklet on practice)

沈洪训 Shen, Hongxun (private publication), 天山五息功 *Tianshan Wuxigong/Five Breathings Practice of the Heavenly Mountains* (book on practice and theory)

沈洪训，夏庭玉 Shen, Hongxun and Xia Tingyu (private publication by Taiji Wuxigong Yanjiuhui in 1986), 太极五息功 *Taiji Wuxigong/Five Breathings Practice of Taiji*

五息闡微 *Wuxi Chanwei/Explanation of the Details of the Five Breathings* (preface by Gu Zuanshao, 1826)

Bibliography

五息直指 Wuxi Zhizhi/Direct Instructions for the Five Breathings (1935), Shanghai: Shanghai Yihuatang Shan Shuju

曾慥 Zeng, Zao (1990 re-edition of Song text, *Daozang* copy), 道樞 *Daoshu/The Pivot of the Way*, Shanghai: Shanghai Guji Chubanshe

張君房 Zhang, Junfang (1988 re-edition of Song text, *Daozang* copy), 雲笈七籤 *Yunji Qiqian/ Seven Lots from the Bookbag of the Clouds*, Qi-Lu Shushe

張隱菴 Zhang, Yin'an (1983 reprint of Qing work), 黃帝內經素問集注 *Huangdi Neijing Suwen Jizhu/Collected Commentaries on the Plain Questions of the Yellow Emperor's Internal Classic*, Tainan: Wangjia Chubanshe

《中国道教》编辑部 Zhongguo Daojiao Bianjibu/Editing Department of "Chinese Taoism" (1987 bilingual Chinese-English edition), 洞天胜境 *Dongtian Shengjing/Famous Centres of Taoism*, Beijing: Zhongguo Daojiao Xiehui

Bibliography

Western Bibliography

Baynes, Cary F. (translator) (1968/1978 10th reprint): *I Ching or Book of Changes, The Richard Wilhelm Translation*, London/Henley-on-Thames: Routledge & Kegan Paul

Chen, William Y. (1987): *A Guide to Tao-Tsang Chi Yao*, New York: The Institute for Advanced Studies of World Religions

Esposito, Monica (1995), *Il qigong. La nuova scuola taoista delle cinque respirazioni*, Padova: Muzzio

Esposito, Monica (general editor) (2008), *Images of Tibet in the 19th and 20th Centuries*, Paris: École Française d'Extrême-Orient

Hermann, Albert (1966 New Edition with general editor Ginsburg, Norton): *An Historical Atlas of China*, Amsterdam: Djambatan

Kohn, Livia (ed.) (2000): *Daoism Handbook*, Leiden/Boston/Köln: Brill

Kohn, Livia (1987): *Seven Steps to the Tao: Sima Chengzhen's Zuowanglun, Nettetal*: Steyler Verlag – Wort und Werk

Kohn, Livia (ed.) (1989): *Taoist Meditation and Longevity Techniques*, Ann Harbor: Center for Chinese Studies, The University of Michigan

Lagerwey, John (1991): *Der Kontinent der Geister, China im Spiegel des Taoismus, Eine Reise nach Innen*, Olten: Walter-Verlag

Bibliography

Liu, Xun (2009): *Daoist Modern, Innovation, Lay Practice, and the Community of Inner Alchemy in Republican Shanghai*, Cambridge (Massachusetts)/London: Harvard University Asia Center

Maspero, Henri (1971): *Le Taoïsme et les religions chinoises*, Paris: Gallimard

Pregadio, Fabrizio (ed.) (2008): *The Encyclopedia of Taoism (2 Vols.)*, Oxon/New York: Routledge

Pregadio, Fabrizio (2011a): *The Seal of the Unity of the Three, A Study and Translation of the* Cantong qi, *the Source of the Taoist Way of the Golden Elixir*, Mountain View: Golden Elixir Press

Pregadio, Fabrizio (2011b): *The Seal of the Unity of the Three, Vol. 2: Bibliographic Studies on the* Cantong qi*: Commentaries, Essays, and Related Works*, Mountain View: Golden Elixir Press

Schipper, K.M. (1975): *Concordance du Houang-t'ing King, Nei-king et Wai-king*, Paris: École Française d'Extrême-Orient

Schipper, Kristofer and Verellen, Franciscus (ed.) (2004): *The Taoist Canon, A Historical Companion to the* Daozang, Chicago/London: The University of Chicago Press

Shaughnessy, Edward L. (translator) (1996), *I Ching, The Classic of Changes*, New York: Ballantine Books

Bibliography

Soothill, William Edward and Hodous, Lewis (1975): *A Dictionary of Chinese Buddhist Terms*, Taipei: Ch'eng Wen Publishing Company

Strickmann, Michel (1981): *Le Taoïsme du Mao Chan, Chronique d'une Révélation*, Paris: Institut des Hautes Études Chinoises

Unschuld, Paul U. and Tessenow, Hermann (2011): *Huang Di nei jing su wen, An Annotated Translation of Huang Di's Inner Classic – Basic Questions (2 Vols.)*, Berkeley/Los Angeles: University of California Press

Unschuld, Paul U. (translator) (1986), *Nan-Ching, The Classic of Difficult Issues*, Berkeley/Los Angeles/London: University of California Press

Vercammen, Dan K.J. (2003): *Jindan, The Golden Cinnabar, Taoist Internal Alchemy, Volume 1*, Antwerp: Belgian Taoist Association

Vercammen, Dan (1995): "Theory and Practice of Chinese Medicine" in Van Alphen, Jan and Aris, Anthony (ed.), *Oriental Medicine, An Illustrated Guide to the Asian Arts of Healing*, London: Serindia Publications

Vercammen, Dan (2000): *The Way of Qi*, Antwerp: Belgian Taoist Association

Wang, Mu (2011): *Foundations of Internal Alchemy, The Taoist Practice of Neidan*, Mountain View: Golden Elixir Press

Ware, James R. (translator & editor) (1966): *Alchemy, Medicine & Religion in the China of A.D. 320, The Nei P'ien of Ko Hung*, New York: Dover Publications

Bibliography

Watson (translator) (1968): *The Complete Works of Chuang Tzu*, New York and London: Columbia University Press

Wong, Eva (translator) (1990): *Seven Taoist Masters, a Folk Novel of China*, Boston: Shambhala Publications

The Author

Dan KJ Vercammen (º 1960) is a Belgian anthropologist and sinologist, holding a PhD from Ghent University. He is a professor and head of research at Taoist Alchemical Studies Center TASC in Antwerp, Belgium, and lectures and teaches at other international institutes. Being interested in health practices and the workings of body and mind since his childhood, he first took up yoga and pranayama breathing practice in 1972 before adding Chinese martial arts to his curriculum from 1975 onwards. In the early 1980s he stopped practicing yoga and pranayama to focus on the theoretical and practical study of Chinese internal practices. From 1985 onwards he spent a lot of time in China to study with several old masters of the internal martial arts, alchemy and traditional medicine. At the same time he started collaborating with Chinese scholars and collecting written material to support his research and practice. While doing so he became a Taoist alchemist, medical doctor, and internal martial arts expert himself. He has written more than thirty books and articles on Chinese (mainly Taoist) subjects in English, Dutch, and Chinese.

More information about his work can be found on this website: www.taoiststudies.org.

Dan KJ Vercammen is also an artist (painter, calligrapher, poet, and designer). His artistic name is Fei Lingbi and www.7starsstudio.shop is his art website.